If you want to win in the lotteries
and sweepstakes, read

THE LUCKY DREAM
AND
NUMBER BOOK

It tells you how to calculate
your special numbers!

This new and expanded edition has an added chapter that
teaches you how to calculate your lucky numbers by
using "fadic" addition and your birthdate!

A treasure trove of folk beliefs, **THE LUCKY
DREAM AND NUMBER BOOK** also helps you
find the lucky numbers hidden in your name and your
dreams. Here, too, you find:

- *The Book of Fate that tells you how to tell your own
  fortune through numerology*
- *Fortune telling through dreams*
- *Lunar prognostications*
- *Lucky and unlucky days*
- *Love charms*
- *How to choose a mate by reading signs*
- *Table for finding lucky numbers by casting dice*
- *Judging character by bodily features*

THE LUCKY
DREAM
AND
NUMBER
BOOK

Revised Edition:

Robert Andrew

WARNER BOOKS

A Warner Communications Company

TABLE OF CONTENTS

BOOK I

ANALYSIS AND INTERPRETATION
OF DREAMS

All people dream. But most forget their dreams when they awake. Only the most vivid—and sometimes the most terrifying—are transported from the subconscious to the conscious mind.

A dream may be formed from a long-forgotten incident of childhood or an event of yesterday. Every thing that happens in a person's life is stored in a mental filing system which provides the images from which dreams are made.

What dreams are and what they mean are two of mankind's oldest mysteries. Over the centuries, researchers have collected innumerable examples of dreams that foretold future events, predicted or prevented tragedies, signaled good or bad fortune, and so on.

The following list contains many subjects that commonly appear in dreams, along with the interpretations given them by experts.

ACQUAINTANCES. To meet acquaintainces in dreams is a good sign if the meeting is friendly. To dream that you fight with them signifies illness, death or destruction.

ADDER. Dreaming of the adder, the asp and other poisonous snakes means you may acquire riches through marriage to more than one wealthy person.

ADULTERY. If you dream you are committing adultery, you will be faced with great temptation or a strenuous inner struggle. But to dream of resisting the temptation of adultery means you will escape impending danger and conquer your enemies. If a woman dreams her skin has changed color, she will be caught in the act of adultery. A dream of intercourse with a deformed person foretells physical or mental illness.

ADVERSARY. To dream of an enemy in business or love indicates you will overcome him and bring the affair to a quick and favorable conclusion.

AIR. To dream you are breathing clear, sweet air shows that you will be loved and esteemed, even by your present enemies. But cloudly, smoggy air is a sign of future troubles.

ALMONDS. To dream of picking or eating almonds signifies business, financial or personal difficulties.

ALMS. To dream you refuse to give alms to a beggar means you too will know want and misery, but to dream of giving them freely indicates a long, happy, prosperous life.

ANGER. If you lose your temper in dreams, you are prone to make enemies when awake.

ANGLING. To dream you are angling but do not catch anything means you will have trouble obtaining something you want very much.

ANTS. Repeated dreams of ants imply sickness and short life. Flying ants mean a dangerous journey or a bad accident. Common ants, which are diligent and industrious, signal prosperity through hard work. They are also a sign of fertility.

APES. Monkeys and apes are a bad omen.

APPLES. Sweet ripe apples denote joy, pleasure and recreation, especially for virgins. Sour apples signify strife and discord.

ARMS. If a man dreams his arms have grown bigger and stronger, he can expect to become wealthy. If a married woman dreams it, her husband is headed for success in his job, either more money or more authority or both. Hairy arms also denote riches. To dream your right arm is cut off signifies the death of father, son or brother; an amputated left arm means the death of mother, daughter or sister.

ARMED MEN. To see soldiers, police or other armed men in dreams is a sign that your fears will soon vanish. Flying men with guns is a sign of victory. But men coming after you with guns signifies a personal tragedy.

ATTORNEYS. To dream you are conferring with lawyers means you will have little success in business or domestic affairs.

AUTHORITY. It is always good for a man to dream he holds a position of authority. The dream could come true.

BACK. A strong backbone signifies health and happiness. A broken or injured back means the dreamer's enemies will get the better of him.

BALL. To dream of dancing at a ball or watching other dancers means joy and happiness.

BANQUETS. To dream of attending a banquet indicates poverty or hunger.

BARKING DOGS. The barking dogs are your enemies and detractors. If you ignore them they will not bite and you will overcome them.

BARN. A barn full of corn, cattle and grain is a sign of a wealthy marriage and prosperity. You will inherit land and grow rich through smart investments.

BASIN. If a man dreams of eating or drinking from a basin, he will fall in love with a pretty young girl.

BAT. To dream of flying bats is a bad sign.

BATH. If a person dreams he goes into or sees himself in a bath, and the water is too hot or too cold, he will have troubles with one or more members of his family. If he dreams of removing his clothes for a bath, but not actually bathing, the trouble will not amount to much.

BEANS. Eating beans in dreams signifies trouble and dissension.

BEAR. A dream bear means a cruel, audacious and wealthy enemy.

BEARD. If a girl dreams she has a beard, she will soon marry a kind husband. The same dream for a married woman means she will lose her husband. A man who dreams he has grown a beard will succeed in his occupation, but if the dream beard falls apart he will come to disgrace.

BEES. Bees signify profit and gain, but if they sting the dreamer he may lose all his profits. Bees flying about your head mean you are beset with enemies, but if you beat the bees off without being stung you will solve all your problems.

BEETS. To dream of growing or eating beets signifies freedom from serious troubles.

BELLS. To dream of hearing bells can be good or bad. If the bells have a happy, cheerful sound, like the pealing of church bells on a holiday, good news can be expected. But if the bell has a loud, urgent ring, like a doorbell or fire alarm, troubles and disgrace lie ahead.

BELLY. To dream one's belly is bigger and fuller than normal means his family and estate will increase. If he dreams of a thin, shrunken stomach, he will be involved in a bad accident but will escape serious injury. Dreams of a bellyache mean trouble in the family.

BIRDS. Many birds in a dream signify business setbacks and lawsuits. The bigger the birds, the worse the trouble. Birds singing and chirping are a good

10

sign. Birds fighting mean mishaps or distress. If the dream birds fly over your head, certain people are prejudiced against you.

BIRDS' NESTS. To dream of finding a nest is usually a good sign, but if there are no eggs or birds in it you will meet with great disappointment.

BLEEDING. To dream of bleeding from the nose signifies loss of money and goods. Bleeding is generally a bad omen, though it can also signify health and joy.

BLINDNESS. If you dream that you are blind, it would be a good idea to study your business and personal affairs, especially affairs of the heart, to see what has gone wrong. In this way, future mistakes may be avoided and past errors corrected.

BLOOD. To dream of blood can signify sickness if the blood color is pure. If the blood is a rich, bright red, it means wealth will soon flow your way.

BLOSSOMS. A dream of blossoms on flowers and trees is a sign of comfort, contentment and opportunities for recreation.

BOAR. A bachelor who dreams of a wild boar will get a nagging, scolding wife. A girl with a similar dream will wind up with a talkative, tiresome husband, more bore than boar.

BOAT. To dream of boating on clear, calm water is a sign of success and prosperity. If the water turns rough and the boat capsizes, the dreamer faces business or romantic troubles.

BREAD. If the bread you eat every day appears in your dreams, this is a good sign. But to dream of eating an unusual kind of bread is bad.

BRIERS. To dream of being torn by briers or thorns signifies unfulfilled desires. A girl is in love if she dreams she gets pricked while plucking a rose.

11

BRIDGE. A broken or washed-out bridge means business obstructions.

BROWS. If a woman dreams of seeing her own face without eyebrows, this is a sign of poverty.

BULL. To dream that you have been gored or trampled by a bull means you will come to some harm. But if you escape the bull or it does not try to gore you, this is a good omen.

BURGLAR. If burglars enter your dreams and steal something, personal misfortune will follow.

BURIED ALIVE. Being buried alive in dreams is a terrifying experience, but it indicates the dreamer will become wealthy.

BURNS. The man who dreams he has been burned to death will become rich and respected. But if the burns are not fatal in the dream, he will eventually die in disgrace. To feel the heat of flames in a dream signifies great personal danger.

BUSINESS. To dream of business deals means they will not be concluded without difficulties.

BUTCHERS. To dream of butchers slaughtering cattle or cutting up meat on the chopping block signifies danger, personal injury or death to the sick.

CAGE. For a young girl to dream she lets a bird out of a cage is a sign her chastity is in danger.

CAKES. To dream of cakes, either on a table or in a bakery display, implies happiness and prosperity.

CANDLES. A candle that is extinguished in a dream means sickness, sadness and poverty. A brightly burning candle means recovery from sickness and future health. To the unwed, it means marriage is just around the corner. If you dream of unlighted candles, your good deads will be rewarded.

CARDS. To dream of playing cards, dice or other games is usually a good omen. But if the dreamer loses the game, he may suffer temporary reverses before his luck changes.

CARROTS. Carrots are a sign of profit and strength.

CATERPILLARS. Crawling caterpillars signify you may meet misfortune at the hands of people you trust.

CATTLE. Dreams of cattle portend financial loss to the rich, profit to the poor. If the cattle are fat, the dreamer will have a generally prosperous year; if they are lean, hard times are coming.

CHEEKS. To dream of plump, rosy cheeks signifies good health, especially in women; pale, lean cheeks imply sickness and grief.

CHERRIES. Eating ripe, red cherries indicates the dreamer will enjoy deceitful pleasures; sour cherries signify a lot of work will be done for nothing.

CHILD. If a married but childless woman dreams of bearing a child, she will become pregnant soon. If an unmarried woman has such a dream, she should consult her physician about a checkup or else take steps to avoid complications.

CHILDREN. Childless couples who dream of having many children will have great difficulty getting one. A man who sees two or three babies born in his dreams will have business success.

CHURCH. To dream of building a church implies some near or distant relative will become a clergyman. To dream you are sitting in church signifies you are going to get some new clothes. In general, church dreams are good omens and indicate the dreamer has a devout, pious nature.

CLIMB. Climbing a tall tree in dreams means success will be obtained through patience and hard work.

CLOTHES. If a man dreams he has a new suit of

clothes, it means personal honor. Burning clothes signify loss and damage to personal property. Black clothes may mean either sorrow or joy. Dirty clothes are a mark of shame. Worn, tattered clothes mean trouble and sadness. If a man dreams of himself in female dress or a woman sees herself attired as a man, hidden desires are indicated.

CLOUDS. White clouds signify prosperity; high, fast-moving clouds mean a journey to a distant land, the return of an absent friend or relative, or a secret that will soon be revealed. Dark clouds in dreams show a time of storms—anger and violence—is approaching.

COALS. Dead coals on a hearth or barbecue oven, signify business success; live, burning coals warn of possible shame and reproach. The man who dreams of falling into a coal pit will marry a widow.

COCK (ROOSTER). To hear a cock crow in dreams is a sign of prosperity. The unmarried girl who dreams of a cock will soon snare a husband.

COFFIN. To dream of one denotes the death of a close friend or relative.

COMEDY. A funny dream, perhaps recalling a comedy seen on the stage or TV, is a sign of good fortune.

COMETS. Fiery comets or stars with streaming tails warn of impending evil, discord or troubles.

COMPLEXION. If you dream of a beautiful unknown woman with a clear complexion, it is a very good sign. To dream of an unknown person whose complexion is marred by a scar, bruise or disease marks is a sign of danger.

CORN. Corn is a sign of plenty. Dreams of corn in the field, on the table or on the foot all indicate profit and riches.

CROCODILE. If an alligator or crocodile slithers

through your dreams, you have false friends or un-scrupulous enemies who will strike when you least expect it.

CROWN. To dream of wearing a crown signifies honor, pride, dignity or delusions of grandeur.

CROW. Crows, ravens and blackbirds all signal bad luck in dreams. If they caw and croak, so much the worse. The crow is the sign of an adulteress and a thief, perhaps warning of an unfaithful wife or un-trustworthy acquaintance. If the dream crow flies onto the head of a child, the dreamer's child or the children or relatives are in danger.

CRUTCHES. To dream of walking on crutches is a warning of sickness or accidental injury. It may also imply that severe obstacles will prevent the attain-ment of some business or personal goal.

CUCUMBERS. Healthy people who dream of eating cucumbers harbor vain hopes; but to the sick, cucumber dreams are a sign of recovery.

DARK. One of the most common and most fright-ening dreams is of being lost in the dark. The dreamer gropes and stumbles but cannot find his way back to the light. Sometimes he falls. Sometimes he finds himself going up high, twisting stairs and is terrified that he will plunge off into the blackness. These dark dreams stem from deep inner turmoil. Blinded by his emotions, the dreamer cannot see a way out of his troubles.

DEAD. To dream of talking with dead people is a sign of courage and a clear conscience. It takes a brave person to commune with the dead, even in dreams. To dream someone is dead when they are actually alive and well is a warning of great trouble. For one to dream himself dead means he will grow rich and live long.

DEER. To dream of deer is a bad omen. To the

bachelor, it means a quarrel with his girl friend. To the married man or woman, it means a bitter domestic dispute. To the tradesman, it means a fight with creditors. To the seaman, it denotes a stormy voyage; and to the pilot, a rough flight. After watching graceful deer run through your dream, expect an argument with friends, business associates or loved ones. Unless you curb your temper, you will be sorry later.

DEVIL. He who dreams of the devil will make fat profits, though not necessarily through honest transactions. Contrary to popular belief, a devil dream is good luck.

DICE. To dream you have won at dice is a sign that you will inherit money on the unexpected death of a relative or friend. To dream you have lost at dice means you will keep on losing.

DIGGING. The man who digs in his dreams is a hard worker and will prosper. But if the shovel or other digging tools are lost, the dreamer soon will be out of work.

DIRT. To dream of dirt, filth and squalor signifies sickness or dishonor. If you fall in the dirt, you have a guilty conscience, you are ashamed of something you have done, or else you will be the victim of a false friend's treachery.

DISEASE. To dream you have any disease when you actually enjoy good health means you will get a better job, a promotion or pay raise soon.

DITCH. A dream of a deep, wide ditch is a danger sign. If the dreamer falls into the ditch, he must take great care to avoid accidents. If he is a merchant, his store or goods will be in danger of catching fire. To dream of crossing a large ditch on a small plank signifies deceit by lawyers.

DOGS (See also "Barking Dogs"). To dream that a dog attacks you and tears your clothes signifies some enemy is out to get you. If another man's dog licks your hand and fawns on you in a dream, this indicates deceit by some flattering "friend" who will betray you. Barking dogs also indicate enemies, but if you beat them off without being bitten you will also overcome your human foes. To dream of small, friendly dogs is a good sign. Large, vicious dogs are not.

DOLPHIN. To dream of a dolphin swimming in the sea indicates a change in the weather or in your personal fortunes. To dream of a dolphin out of water signifies the impending death of a friend.

DRAGON. A dragon dream is one of the best, signifying sound investments that should make you rich.

DRINK. Drinking soda or alcoholic beverages in dreams is a sign of success in love. The man who dreams he is happily drunk will be loved by a pleasant, attractive and wealthy woman. If you dream you are thirsty, searching for water but unable to find a drop anywhere, you will be unable to conclude an important business venture; but if you find water to appease your thirst, the deal will be concluded successfully. Drinking cold water is a sign of health and long life; hot water signifies sickness and career difficulties.

DROWN. To dream of drowning is a warning of impending tragedy, possibly even death; but if you are rescued from drowning in the dream, you will overcome misfortune.

EAGLE. To dream of an eagle high in the sky is a good sign, especially for those engaged in difficult or dangerous work, such as combat soldiers or policemen. But if an eagle lights on the dreamer's head, this is a sign of death.

EAR. If a man dreams he has small, well-shaped ears, he will be liked and respected. If he dreams his ears are large or malformed, he will be scorned and despised. A dream of an itchy ear is a portent of good news. An ear that is cut, bleeding or bruised means the dreamer wil be offended by someone close to him. If he dreams an ear is cut off, he will lose a close friend or relative.

EARTH. A dream of fertile land or an attractive, fenced-in lot is the sign of a good marriage, children and prosperity. But parched or blackened earth signifies sorrow and mental or moral weakness.

EARTHQUAKE. If you dream the earth is trembling, there will be a change in your job or personal affairs. A dream of a great quake that opens deep chasms in the earth signifies personal injuries, death or loss of property. To dream that an earthquake causes your walls, doors and roof to cave in means death to the head of the family.

EARTHWORMS. To dream of earthworms signifies secret enemies who are trying to ruin you.

ECLIPSE. For one to dream of the sun in eclipse signifies the loss of his father; the moon in eclipse denotes the death of his mother; if the dreamer has neither father nor mother, than the eclipse means the death of some other relative.

EGGS. For doctors, artists and tradesmen, a dream of eggs is a sign of profits. For others, eggs mean pain, noise and lawsuits. Broken eggs signify great personal loss.

ELEPHANT. An elephant signifies long life and prosperity.

ENEMY. To dream you are talking to an enemy, or to a friend who appears in the dream as an enemy, is a warning to beware of him.

EVIL SPIRITS. If monsters or other weird apparitions appear in your dreams, your affairs will be obstructed by a hypocritical person and you will learn some terrible truths that you never suspected.

EXECUTIONS. To dream of a criminal being executed, or of a gallows, gas chamber, electric chair or other place of executions, means someone with serious troubles will appeal to you for help. If the dreamer sees himself executed, he is about to be punished for past deeds.

EYEBROWS. If the dreamer sees his eyebrows change, giving him a more attractive appearance, this is a sign of romance and marriage.

EYES. If one dreams he has lost his eyesight, it means he will break a promise or lose a friend whom he will never see again. A dream of blurred vision that suddenly clears signifies the dreamer will commit a crime and regret it. To dream of sharp, clear, far-seeing eyes is an extraordinary sign, meaning success in nearly all enterprises. Sore, swollen eyes in dreams denote sickness.

FACE. A pretty, smiling face signifies friendship and joy. A pale, sad face is a sign of trouble, poverty or death. If the dreamer observes himself washing his own face, this signifies repentance for sin.

FAIR. To dream of attending a fair, circus, carnival or other large public gathering is a warning to watch your wallet.

FALL. If one falls down in a dream and is unable to get up, the dreamer will lose the favor of someone he admires and will be unable to regain it. But if he gets up after a fall, he will be restored to favor after a temporary estrangement. Falling from a roof, window or other high place indicates mental depression. It may also denote a sudden loss.

FEAST. A dream of feasting with friends or relatives is a good, auspicious sign.

FEET. Washing the feet in dreams portends troubles. Scratching the feet means the dreamer will be tricked through flattery.

FIELDS. To dream of pleasant, tree-shaded fields, parks and meadows is a good omen. To a man, it means he has or will soon have a beautiful wife who will bear him handsome children. To a woman, it means a thoughtful, kind and devoted husband.

FIGHTING. Fight dreams signal strife, domestic discord or career conflicts; if the dreamer is injured in a fight, he faces loss of reputation.

FIGS. Eating figs or dates in dreams is a sign of happiness.

FINGERS. Cut fingers portend damage. To dream you lose one or more fingers means you will hurt or lose friends. To dream one has more fingers than usual signifies a deadbeat who would rather owe than pay.

FIRE (See also "Burns"). Dreams of fire and flames are warnings of imminent danger.

FISH (See also "Angling"). Catching large fish in dreams means profitable investments or business deals. Catching dead fish means your enterprises will fail. A pregnant woman who dreams she delivers a fish instead of a child will lose her baby. To dream of dead fish floating in the water signifies false hopes. The dreamer who catches small, worthless fish is wasting his time on some project. Red fish are a sign of sickness; fish of many colors denote sickness, injury and grief.

FLEAS. Hopping, jumping fleas indicate the dreamer has jittery nerves and should seek calmer surroundings.

FLESH. To dream of naked male or female flesh signifies sexual desire. If one dreams his own flesh is ~~asing, he will gain wealth. If he loses weight ~~rows thin in dreams, financial losses are indicated. To dream of eating large quantities of flesh, either animal, fowl or fish, signifies neglect of business or mistakes made through anger.

FLIES. Swarming flies mean you are bothered by enemies or unreasonable people whose actions upset you.

FLOODS. Great floods, sweeping away everything in their path, indicate crowds of people, loud noise, discord and violence. To dream of escaping from a flood signifies you will overcome formidable obstacles.

FLOWERS. Gathering, holding and smelling flowers in dreams denote joy and happiness if the flowers are in season. The dreamer adorned with garlands of flowers will have a pleasant experience which will not last long. White flowers, appearing out of season, imply business obstacles; yellow flowers have a similar meaning but indicate the obstacles are small; red flowers signify extreme difficulties which could result in death.

FLUTE. To dream of playing or listening to a flute signifies inner turmoil, perhaps of a sexual nature.

FLYING. Dreams of flight generally signify escape from problems, release from pain or sickness, a long journey, adventures in foreign lands. The dreamer who is flying aboard a plane or with wings of his own is emerging from a difficult period. Plane-crash dreams portend personal or business disaster. If the dreamer sees himself flying through the air without wings, this is a sign of fear and danger.

FOOLISH. If a young woman dreams she has done something foolish, she will marry an honest man; if a married woman dreams she is guilty of folly, her first or next child will be a boy; if a man dreams he is a fool, he is wise enough to know his shortcomings and profit by them.

FOREST. To dream of walking in a vast, trackless forest signifies troubles, possibly financial problems.

FORTUNE. Dreams of fortune are usually good. If a wealthy man loses his money, then dreams he has all his former possessions, he will make another fortune.

FOUNTAIN. A dream fountain, gushing clear water, is a very favorable sign. It implies love, a happy marriage, a successful career. But if the water is muddy, you can expect disappointment in business, an unfaithful sweetheart, a broken marriage.

FOX. A man who dreams of a fox has either a shrewd, crafty business adversary or a quick-tempered, shrewish wife. A woman who dreams of a fox will take an unfaithful husband or lover.

FRIENDS. To dream of friends is generally good. To dream a living friend is dead means the dreamer is neglecting his pals. To dream a sweetheart is dead means the romance is over. The arrival of friends means deliverance from trouble.

FROGS. The frog is a lucky omen.

FRUIT. Gathering or eating ripe fruit in dreams signifies great profit; but if the fruit tastes rotten or sour, the profits will soon be gone.

GAMES. To dream of vigorous athletic games—baseball, football, tennis, etc.—implies good health, ambition and success in most undertakings.

GARDEN (See also "Flowers"). The bachelor who dreams of a lovely garden will marry a beautiful and virtuous girl. The spinster who dreams of gardens will soon meet the right man.

GIANT. The Jolly Green Giant and other huge figures are generally good omens in dreams. But if you dream that a giant is chasing you, troubles are closing in.

GIFTS. To dream of giving away something of

value is a sign of loss, though it may also signify a new romance. To dream of receiving a gift signifies happiness.

GLASS. A glass full of clear water signifies a good marriage with several children. If the dreamer sees his own reflection in a glass or mirror, and the image is untrue, this is a sign of infidelity in a loved one.

GLOVES. Wearing gloves in dreams signifies safety, security or a suspicious nature.

GOATS. To dream of goats is a sign of wealth and plenty.

GOLD. Gold coins and jewelry denote good fortune. If a man dreams he is gathering up gold, he should beware of deceit. To dream of giving away gold means you will receive bad news, but to dream you receive it means good news is coming. If a man dreams a gold tooth is being yanked from his mouth, his wife or friends will get all his money.

GRAIN. Gathering grain in dreams signifies a harvest of good profits.

GRAPES. White grapes indicate gain; black or purple grapes indicate loss.

GROUND. If a person falls on the ground in a dream, dishonor, shame and scandal will follow.

HAIL. To dream of a hail storm signifies sorrow and trouble; the bigger the hailstones, the worse the trouble. Hail also means you will find out what your partner has been trying to conceal from you.

HAIR. If a man dreams he has long, flowing hair, he will display cowardice, effeminacy and will be deceived by a woman. A woman who dreams of losing her hair will lose her husband or a close friend. A bald woman in dreams signifies hunger, poverty and sickness. A bald man signals wealth, health and abundance. If you have hair but dream you are bald, you are ashamed of something you have done. If you are bald but dream you have hair, you will be successful in love.

HANDS. If you dream your hands are better formed or stronger than they really are, you will accomplish an important task. To dream of a severed, burned or disfigured hand signifies impending poverty or loss of a loved one. Excessively hairy hands mean troubles that could lead to imprisonment.

HANG. Dreams of hanging are nightmares with happy endings. If the dreamer sees himself hanged or condemned to the gallows, he will be rich and respected. But if, in the dream, he is saved by a last-minute reprieve, he will lose his money and dignity. Similar conclusions can be drawn from other dreams about capital punishment.

HARPIES. Dreams of shrieking monsters with the faces of women and the bodies of snakes or birds mean the dreamer will be ruined by envious, greedy persons, possibly in his own family.

HATE. To dream of hatred or being hated is a bad sign.

HEAD. A person who dreams his head has grown to a very large size will attain a position of authority, though it may cost him friends. If a dreamer sees his own head cut off, he will suffer great loss. This may mean death of a husband, wife, child, other relative or loss of property. If you dream of cutting off another person's head, you will succeed in your projects even though ruthless means may be necessary. Cutting off a chicken's head signifies pleasure and recreation. If the dreamer washes his own head, this signifies deliverance from danger.

HEAVEN. To dream of ascending to Heaven signifies happiness and peace of mind.

HEN (See also "Cock"). A hen laying eggs portends financial gain. A hen with her chickens implies loss and damage. A crowing hen warns of sorrow and trouble. To dream you are turned into a hen indicates sexual inadequacy.

HILLS. When a dreamer sees himself climbing high, steep hills or mountains, he can expect to encounter great difficulties but will overcome them with common sense and good counsel.

HOG'S BRISTLES. To dream hog's bristles are sprouting from your face is a sign of sudden and violent danger.

HORNETS. A dream of hornets means you will have to deal with people who will try to discredit you.

HORSES. In general, a horse is a sign of good luck. A running horse signifies prosperity and accomplishment. To dream of riding a tired horse indicates you will fall desperately in love. A dead horse means your business or job will stagnate and you will suffer financial losses, but the situation will not become desperate. A horse race denotes a quick profit.

HOUSE. To dream of building a house is a sign of marriage, success and contentment. A burning house is a bad sign. To dream of setting fire to a house or watching it burn means you will be involved in scandal. To dream the top of your house is on fire signifies the death of your marriage partner or a friend's mate.

HUNGER. To dream of an abnormal hunger indicates wealth will be obtained through hard work, ambition and ingenuity.

HUNTING. If you dream of hunting and killing a fox, a false friend will get you in trouble, but you will discover the treachery in time to prevent disaster. If the fox gets away, you will be betrayed so subtly that you may never realize what happened. If you dream of hunting a rabbit, you will be disappointed in your most important endeavors. If you dream of killing a deer, you will lose a close friend. But if the deer escapes alive, you will prosper.

HUSBAND. If a woman dreams of her husband but cannot see his face, or if he has a different face, she will betray him. If an unmarried woman dreams of a husband, she will find one soon. If a woman dreams of someone else's husband, scandal and despair will result.

HYMN. To dream of singing a hymn signifies a business venture will be hindered.

ICE. A dream of ice, in a glass or on the ground, indicates you will have hardships to overcome but they will eventually melt away.

INDIANS. An attack by Indians, a recurrent theme in many American dreams, indicates some of your associates will try to dishonor or discredit you. To dream of being shot in the back by an Indian arrow means your sweetheart or spouse is unfaithful. If the dreamer is scalped by Indians, he will lose his reputation. If he sees himself as an Indian, scalping a fallen foe, he will overcome a rival in business or love.

INK. Dreams of ink are usually associated with business troubles. Red ink signals a commercial or financial disaster. Black or blue ink implies prosperity. Ink flowing from a pen signifies sickness and death.

JEEP. To dream of riding in a jeep over rough terrain means you will have to overcome many hardships before your ultimate goal is obtained.

JETS (See also "Flying"). To dream of a jet plane taking off with a great roar signifies recreation, adventure, escape from problems. But a jet that takes off silently and flies without a sound is a bad omen.

In general, dreams of jet aircraft imply travel and romance.

KEYS. If you dream of losing your keys, you will lose your temper and quarrel with a friend. To a prisoner, a dream of keys indicates he will soon be released. To a bachelor or spinster, keys signify marriage. To a detective, scientist or laboratory technician, a key means the solving of a mystery.

KILL. To dream you kill a man assures success in a business or financial venture. If you dream of killing a stranger, you will "make a killing" at the racetrack or stock market. To dream of killing your wife, husband or sweetheart means suspected infidelity. To dream of killing your mother or father is bad. If you dream you are being murdered, and the killer is someone you know, he will suffer personal or business loss.

KISS. If a man dreams of kissing a pretty girl who vanishes before he can fulfill his desire, the next day will be a happy one for him. Dreams of kisses and embraces signify strife or sexual frustration. To dream of kissing a dead person signifies long life.

KITE. To dream of flying a kite means escape from danger.

KNIFE. A dream of a knife or knives portends a quarrel with friends or acquaintances, but it will end peacefully.

LADDER. To ascend a ladder in dreams signifies success; to descend a ladder signifies failure. Walking under a ladder indicates you will be tricked into making a wrong move.

LAMB. A lamb or baby goat signifies a comfortable life. But if you dream of killing a lamb, your mind is troubled because you have deceived a loved one.

LAND (See also "Earth" and "Fields"). A dream of spacious, enclosed land signifies a good marriage.

If the land is not enclosed, this indicates pleasure and riches. If a man dreams of unenclosed lands containing woods, gardens, fields and a pond, stream or swimming pool, he will marry a beautiful, faithful woman who will bear him handsome, intelligent children.

LAUREL. A laurel tree is a sign of pleasure and plenty. If a woman dreams she sees or smells laurel, she will bear children.

LAW. Dreams of legal proceedings, courtrooms, lawyers, judges, etc. signify trouble, expense and secrets revealed. If a sick man dreams of winning a lawsuit, he will soon recover.

LEGS. Long, shapely legs signify happiness and a prosperous trip or business venture. To dream your legs itch indicates frustration. If you dream you have an artificial leg, this is a warning of bad times ahead.

LEOPARD. A leopard signifies pride and honor.

LETTERS. To dream of writing to friends or of receiving letters from them means good news is on the way.

LETTUCE. Dreaming of eating lettuce in a sandwich or salad signifies you will have difficulty managing your affairs.

LICE. Large numbers of lice or roaches signify sickness, poverty or imprisonment. But if the dreamer kills all the bugs, he will overcome his troubles.

LIGHT. A lighted window in the dark signifies safety and security, but if the light suddenly goes out, leaving the dreamer in the dark, misfortune is indicated. A distant light seen from a ship, plane, car or train means the successful completion of a long trip or project.

LIGHTNING. Lightning flashes without thunder indicate the dreamer will change his job, address or position in life. Lightning bolts also signify a marital split, ending in divorce, or friends turned to enemies. For bachelors and spinsters, distant lightning signals approaching marriage. If a married woman dreams of a tree split by lightning, she will lose a child or children. If the dreamer sees himself hit by lightning, he will die.

LILIES. To dream one sees, holds or smells lilies in season (generally spring and summer) signifies the successful accomplishment of an important project. Lilies out of season indicate frustration and failure.

LION. A lion is a good omen, signifying strength and power. To dream of hunting or fighting a lion indicates great difficulties but they will be overcome if the dream lion is killed.

LIPS. If a man dreams of a woman's full, red lips, he will have an extremely passionate affair. Red, handsome lips indicate good health; pale, chapped or cracked lips signify illness and weakness. A woman who dreams her lips are larger and more attractive than usual is about to embark on a romantic adventure.

LIZARD. A lizard signifies bad luck and treachery by false friends.

LOGS. To dream of splitting logs or stacking logs in front of a fireplace means a stranger will call at your house.

LOST. If a person dreams of searching for lost articles—money, clothing, jewelry, etc.—he is entering a period of great uncertainty, tension and anxiety. A woman who dreams she has lost her wedding ring has little love for her husband, but a woman who dreams her lost wedding ring has been found will have a reconciliation with her husband after a marital break or separation.

LUST. Dreams of lust and lechery indicate frustrated desire or sexual inadequacy. If a man dreams of taking a woman by force, he will be driven to desperate measures in an effort to prove himself.

LYING. The person who dreams of telling lies will deceive his loved ones, friends or business associates. But if the dreamer is a professional actor or comedian, the dream indicates he will give outstanding performances.

MAIL (See also "Letters"). Mail from friends portends good news. Business mail means an increase in your work load. An envelope with a black border signifies bad news. If the dreamer sees himself delivering mail, he will make many friends and business connections.

MARRIAGE. To dream you are getting married is a warning of danger. A dream of a formal wedding signifies the death or sudden departure of a friend.

MEASLES. If a person dreams he has the measles, he will make money by deceitful or dishonest means.

MELONS. Ripe melons, on the vine or on the table, signify good fortune and prosperity. A sick person who dreams of eating melons will soon get well. But a melon that suddenly turns black and rotten signifies sickness.

MILK. To dream of milk is a very good sign. If a women dreams her breasts are swollen with milk, she will marry a wealthy man or, if already married, will soon become pregnant. Spilled milk, however, is a sign of misfortune.

MONEY. To dream of losing money means your fortunes will improve after a brief setback; to dream of finding money means a quick profit that will be spent just as quickly.

MONKEY. A dream of monkeys indicates some of your acquaintances are malicious enemies.

MONSTERS. Sea monsters are a sign of evil, but all other kinds of dream monster signify good luck.

MOON. A bright or full moon signifies a kind, loving marriage partner; dark clouds drifting across the face of the moon indicate sickness or a loved one's financial reverses or a dangerous journey. If a darkened moon becomes bright again, the dreamer will overcome serious hardships. If the dreamer sees a face in the moon, this signifies romance, marriage or childbirth.

MOTHER. If a dreamer sees his mother alive, this is a sign of good luck; if he sees his mother dead, misfortune will follow.

MOUNTAINS. To dream of mountains, valleys, woods and plains is a sign of tremendous obstacles to overcome. Climbing a high mountain indicates a tough struggle to reach the top in your career. Falling from a mountain peak is a warning of disaster.

MOUTH. A big mouth is a symbol of prosperity; a small mouth implies caution and temerity. If the dreamer sees his mouth grow large, he and his family will prosper.

MULBERRY TREE. To dream of a mulberry tree denotes an abundance of children and possessions.

MUSIC. Dreaming of pleasant music is a sign that good news will soon be received; loud, harsh, discordant music signifies the opposite.

MYRTLE TREE. In dreams, myrtle trees signify a wanton woman. If the dreamer sees a myrtle tree, this indicates an unfaithful spouse or sweetheart.

NAILS. To dream that one's fingernails are longer than usual signifies profit; short nails denote loss. If the dreamer sees his nails cut off, he will suffer loss and disgrace and will have bitter quarrels with friends and relations. If his nails are pulled out, this signifies misery, sickness and danger of death. Nail-biting in dreams shows a nervous, quarrelsome nature; nail-polishing and paring means a long illness.

NAKEDNESS. If a woman dreams of seeing her husband or boy friend naked, she will have success in her endeavors. If she dreams of a strange man naked, this is a sign of terror or suppressed desire. For a man to dream of a beautiful naked woman is a sign of joy and prosperity. But if she is ugly, wrinkled and deformed, this signifies shame, remorse and bad luck. The dreamer who sees himself naked faces loss of virtue, honor or wealth.

NAVIGATION. To dream of sailing a boat or piloting a plane denotes that the dreamer is capable of managing his own affairs. If the water is rough or the air turbulent, this means difficulties to overcome. Shipwreck and plane crash dreams warn of danger or death.

NIGHTBIRDS. Dreams of owls, bats and other night-flying creatures are ominous signs. People who experience such dreams should refrain from making important decisions, taking trips or conducting risky business on the following day. If such a dream occurs while the dreamer is away from home on business or vacation, he should beware of thieves.

NIGHTMARE. This is the term for a particularly disturbing, terrifying or horrible dream. But such dreams are not necessarily bad omens. Many frightful dreams signify good luck, prosperity, happiness and success. Nightmares frequently shock dreamers into an awareness of reality, so that they can take steps to avoid or correct a dangerous situation.

NOSE. To dream of growing a large nose is a sign of profits through dealings with wealthy persons; a shrinking nose signifies loss and misfortune; an itchy nose means good news.

NUTS. To dream of cracking and eating nuts signifies contentment gained after hard labor and pain.

OFFICE. To dream of working in a large office

is a sign of many friends; to dream of having your own large executive office means you will work hard to gain prestige and then struggle even harder to keep it.

OIL. For a woman to dream of fragrant oils, lotions, creams and other cosmetics means she is in danger of losing her beauty or of losing someone who found her beautiful. If a man dreams of gushing oil wells, he will gain unexpected wealth; if he dreams oil is leaking from his car or heating system, he will invest money foolishly and lose it.

OLD PEOPLE. To dream of marrying a much older person is a sign of accomplishment in business affairs.

ONIONS. If a person dreams he eats or smells onions, garlic, leeks, etc., he will learn an unpleasant secret and this will lead to domestic strife.

ORANGES. Oranges, whether ripe or rotten, signify grief, troubles and wounds to the body or spirit.

ORCHARDS. Dreams of apple, peach and cherry orchards denote pleasure and prosperity. A great orchard full of fruit-laden trees indicates wealth, comfort and recreation. But if the trees are bare, without fruit or leaves, the dreamer will fail to attain his goals in life.

OVEN. A hot oven implies change of position or place. If a person dreams of being burned by or in an oven, he will make a change for the worse.

OWLS (See also "Nightbirds"). Owls are a bad sign.

OYSTERS. To dream of opening and eating oysters signifies a long voyage and sexual fulfillment.

PALM. The palm tree is a sign of pleasure, adventure and romance. If a woman dreams of sitting under a palm tree, she will soon be married or, if already married, will become pregnant. If a man dreams of sitting under a palm tree and being hit on the head with a coconut, he will profit from a sudden inspiration.

PAPER. To read or write on a paper indicates important news is coming. If the paper is smudged or torn, your affairs will go well.

PARTRIDGES and PHEASANTS. The man who dreams of hunting partridges and pheasants will chase many women, but the ones he catches will be malicious, ungrateful and unfaithful.

PEACHES. A dream of peaches is an omen of health and fortune.

PEACOCK. A man who dreams of seeing a peacock will marry a beautiful woman; a woman who dreams of seeing a peacock will marry a vain, arrogant, selfish man. One who dreams of himself as a peacock will lose friends through self-conceit.

PEARS. A dream of pears is an omen of business success.

PICTURES. To dream of drawing or taking pictures signifies pleasure without profit; if the dreamer sees himself being drawn, painted or photographed, he will enjoy a long, full life.

PIGEONS. Pigeon dreams are generally good, but the person who dreams of himself as a pigeon will cause trouble and heartbreak to those who care for him.

PLANTS. Plants, vines, flowers and trees signify an active life marked by constant change and rapid developments, both good and bad. To dream a plant is growing out of your body is a sign of death.

PLAY. To dream of watching a comedy, musical or other amusing play denotes success in love or business. To dream of viewing a tragedy in the movies, on the stage or on TV signifies hard work, loss, grief and affliction.

POOL. If a man dreams of a pool, pond or small lake, he will be loved by a beautiful woman. If a woman has such a dream, she will attain her desires. But if the pool or pond is dry, the dreamer will be unable to bear children. A dried-up pond also signifies sickness and death. A dream of boating on a placid pond signifies joy and success. A dream of diving into an empty swimming pool portends death or disaster.

PORTRAIT. If a man dreams he is gazing at the portrait, statue or photograph of a beautiful nude woman, he will have good luck. If a woman dreams of posing for a nude portrait, she will have many lovers.

POVERTY. To dream of poverty means you will suffer many hardships and will never find happiness even if you become wealthy.

PRISON. One who dreams of convicts and prison has a clear conscience, unless he sees himself among the prisoners.

PURSE. If a woman dreams of losing an old, empty purse, she will soon have a new one, full of money. If she dreams of losing a purse full of cash, she will become involved with a cheating man. And if she dreams her purse is stolen, her husband or lover will run off with another woman.

QUAGMIRE. To dream of falling into a bog, swamp or quagmire signifies involvement in personal or business difficulties.

QUARRELS. Quarrels and arguments in dreams portend unexpected pleasure.

QUEEN. A woman who dreams she is a queen will have many suitors but will reject the one who could make her happy. Queens and kings in dreams generally denote wealth and high position.

RACE. To dream of a foot race, horse race or auto

race is an auspicious sign unless the race ends in tragedy, in which case bad luck is indicated.

RADISHES. Radishes signify a loud, violent quarrel, probably a domestic spat.

RAIN. A light shower in dreams means pleasure and profit. But a heavy rain, accompanied by thunder, lightning, hail and high winds, means trouble and peril.

RAINBOW. To dream of a rainbow in the sky is a good sign. If you find a pot of gold at the end of it, so much the better.

RICE. The person who dreams of consuming large quantities of rice will learn a lot and profit by his knowledge.

RIDING. To dream of riding in a car or train is a good sign if the journey is pleasant. If the ride is rough and unpleasant, the dreamer will realize his ambition only after many obstacles are overcome.

RING. Rings signify friendship, love, marriage.

RIOT. To dream of watching or participating in a riot means you are surrounded by enemies intent on damaging your career or reputation.

RIVER. A calm, clear river signifies a pleasant, comfortable life with few worries. A wild, turbulent river indicates future danger. If the dreamer is caught in a strong current and unable to reach shore, he is attempting more than he can accomplish.

ROSES. Picking or smelling roses in dreams is a good omen. If a thorn cuts the dreamer as he plucks a rose, and if blood drops from the wound, this means great success will be attained after a hard struggle.

RUN. If a man is running away from something in a dream, he is afraid of his wife, boss, job, etc. If a man is running after something, he is in a great hurry to get ahead. If he wants to run but cannot lift his feet, he has a great desire to accomplish something but lacks the ability.

SALT. To dream of tasting salt signifies good luck.

SEA. A dream of walking on the sea is a favorable omen for travelers, persons involved in lawsuits and people contemplating marriage. To a young man, this dream means he will win the love of a delightful woman. To a young woman, the same dream means she is living a dissolute, immoral life, "for the sea is like a harlot, having a fair appearance but bringing many to an evil end." To dream of drowning in the sea signifies death or ruin, but rescue from drowning indicates a narrow escape from danger.

SEABIRDS. Dreams of gulls, pelicans and other seabirds indicate a long journey or the loss of a close friend.

SEAT. Falling out of a seat signifies loss of a job or position. If the dreamer cannot regain his seat, the loss will be permanent.

SHEEP. Dreams of sheep, cows, horses and other farm animals are generally good. If a sheep is being sheared, the wool indicates wealth. But if the dreamer sees himself as a newly-shorn sheep, he will be cheated out of his money by someone he trusted.

SHIPS. Passenger liners and cruise ships signify pleasure, recreation, romance; cargo ships loaded with goods indicate prosperity; a ship pounded by towering waves and high winds is a sign of danger; a sinking ship means tragedy or death.

SHOES. To dream of losing one's shoes and walking barefoot signifies foot pains and sickness. If this dream should come during the new moon, it also denotes loss and self-reproach.

SHOOTING. (See also "Hunting"). Shooting game in dreams is a favorable sign. To the lover, it portends a delightful conquest; to the broker, banker and merchant, success and riches; to the sailor, soldier and marine, wealth acquired in a distant land. But if you dream you fire many shots without killing any game, this signals disappointment in business and love.

SHOWER. (See also "Rain"). To dream of a rain shower, without thunder or wind, is a good sign.

SICKNESS. To dream one is sick signifies idleness and unemployment. To dream of comforting the sick denotes profit from good works.

SILVER. To dream of gathering silver coins or silver jewelry signifies loss through deceit.

SINGING. If a person dreams he is singing, he will soon be sad. To dream of listening to singing denotes consolation during a time of sorrow, but if a sick person dreams of hearing songs it means recovery of health. To hear birds sing signifies love, joy and delight.

SNOW. To dream of snow signifies temporary setbacks in your job, career or business. To a traveler or soldier, snow indicates plans will be frustrated.

SOLDIERS. Dreams about soldiers imply troubles and adversity.

SON. If a man dreams of talking to his son, he will suffer unexpected damage.

SPIDERS. Spiders and scorpions portend bad luck.

SPIRITS. Dreams of spirits, ghosts and phantoms are not uncommon even in this enlightened age. If the spirits are transparent or white, this signifies joy and pleasure. If they are dark and deformed, this means deceit and temptation to sin.

SQUIRREL. If a man dreams he has a pet squirrel, he will be lured into a love affair or marriage with a spiteful, bad-natured woman; if a woman dreams of feeding squirrels, she will be seduced by unfaithful men.

STARS. To dream of bright, clear stars is a good

sign, indicating prosperity, good news or a pleasant journey. But if the stars are pale and blurred, troubles lie ahead. If the stars go out, leaving the sky black and blank, there will be serious difficulties or even death.

STATUES. To dream of statues is a generally favorable omen. If the dreamer sees himself as a statue, long life is indicated. Statues that seem to come alive and move about denote unexpected riches.

STINGS. If you dream you are stung by a bee, wasp or other insect, grief and deceit will upset your plans. To some, a painful sting means love turned to hatred.

STONES. If the dreamer sees himself walking on stones or in a place where stones are lying all around, many hardships are in store.

STRANGERS. To dream of being among strangers, without seeing a familiar face, means a complete change of job, environment or circumstances.

SUN. The sun is a very good omen, signifying advancement to a desired goal. A bright, clear sun indicates happiness, health and accomplishment, but if clouds cover the sun there is danger ahead. To dream of the sun and moon together is a bad sign. A dream of a sunrise predicts good news, but a sunset means sorrow.

SWALLOW. To dream of a swallow is a favorable sign if the bird does not fly away. If the swallow flies from sight, misfortune is indicated.

SWAN. A swan floating on water denotes joy, health and happiness to the dreamer, but a singing swan means death.

SWEETHEART. If a man dreams of a sweetheart far away and she is smiling and more beautiful than ever, this means she has been faithful during his absence; if she looks pale, nervous and ashamed, she is running around with other men.

SWELLING. To dream of swellings in the arms, legs, head or body signifies sudden wealth.

SWIMMING. A dream of swimming or wading in water is good as long as the head is above the surface; if the head goes under, it is a dangerous dream signifying loss, discord or a broken marriage.

SWORD. To dream of a naked sword or a sword fight indicates anger and a violent quarrel which will be quickly settled without any lasting animosity.

TABLE. A table loaded with food and drink is a sign of plenty and prosperity; an empty dining table denotes poverty.

TEETH. To dream of losing your teeth signifies loss of friends or prestige; if your teeth are being pulled out, you will lose money through bad investments; false teeth denote false friends, bad advice or death.

THIGHS. For a woman to dream her thighs are hot and feverish means she will have an affair with a stranger; in a married woman, this dream means loss of her husband through death or divorce. A dream of large, powerful thighs is a sign of fertility and prosperity.

THIRST. If a person dreams he has a great thirst, he is ambitious and will achieve success, though not necessarily happiness.

THORNS (See also "Roses"). To dream of walking on thorns indicates you will triumph over adversity.

THROAT. If a person dreams his throat has been cut, he will be injured by someone he knows. If he dreams of cutting another person's throat, he will do himself some great injury. A dry, parched throat is a warning of danger.

THUNDER. A dream of thunder indicates a

change in job or status that will not be as significant as it first seems.

TOMB. To dream of building a tomb signifies a marriage or birth of children. In general, a tomb dream is a good omen but if the tomb appears neglected and falling to ruin it signifies sickness and destruction.

TOP. If you dream of spinning a child's top you will endure pains and hardships but will profit from your misfortune.

TORCH. For a young person to dream of holding a burning torch is a good sign, signifying a full life, pleasant love affairs, accomplishments and promotions. To dream of seeing a blazing torch suddenly go out means sadness because of sickness or death.

TRAVELING. A swift, pleasant journey indicates a comfortable life with no great hardships. If one dreams he is traveling through a dark forest and is caught by briers, bushes and branches, he will have many troubles and problems. To travel over high hills and mountains indicates great difficulties will be overcome. To dream of traveling in a jet plane or space craft signifies the dreamer is willing to take risks in order to accomplish his goals.

TREASURE. To dream of finding buried treasure is a very bad omen.

TREES. Planting trees in dreams signifies a good marriage and children; chopping down trees indicates loss; trees bearing fruit, leaves or flowers signify financial success; withered trees indicate deceit; climbing a tree means you will attain an important position; falling from a tree is a warning of disaster.

UMBRELLA. If you dream of holding an umbrella over your head during a shower, you will pass up several opportunities because you are too cautious. A dream of an open umbrella indoors implies sickness.

UNDERWEAR. A man who dreams of walking outdoors or appearing before others in his undershorts will be deceived by a loved one. A woman who dreams of appearing in public in her panties and bra will make a foolish mistake due to love.

VINE. Vines, especially clinging vines, indicate romance, fertility and a large family.

VINEGAR. To dream you drink or bathe in vinegar signifies illness.

VIRGIN. The girl who dreams of losing her virginity is in danger of doing just that. A dream of the Holy Virgin signifies peace of mind, recovery from sickness and tranquility.

WALKING. To dream of walking in dirt or mud signifies shame. Walking in water or a heavy rain signifies adversity and grief; walking in the dark, without stars or a light, indicates trouble or danger.

WAR. To dream of war is a bad sign except to military men who will profit from such an omen.

WASHING. A dream of washing or bathing is generally good, implying health, prosperity and a clear conscience. If a person dreams he is taking a bath with his clothes on, this signifies sickness or danger.

WATER. Clear, calm water is a good omen; dark, turbulent water is not.

WEDDINGS. If a woman dreams of watching her own wedding, she will be unlucky in love; if a sick man dreams he is getting married to a pretty young girl, he will soon die; to dream of marrying a deformed person indicates contentment in life; to dream of marrying a handsome man or woman denotes happiness.

WEEPING. For a person to dream of weeping and sorrow is a sign of great joy and mirth.

WIFE. If a man dreams his wife has married someone else, this signifies change of affairs or conditions.

The same holds true for a woman who dreams her husband has remarried.

WINE. To dream of drinking good wine implies health and success. Sour wine signifies involvement with a cheap, scheming person.

WOUNDS. Stomach wounds signify good news; heart wounds, an unfaithful mate or sweetheart; head wounds, someone is picking your brains for his own advantage; body wounds, money earned the hard way.

X-RAY. If the dreamer seems to be studying X-ray pictures of himself, this signifies a clear conscience and untroubled mind.

YOUTH. If an elderly person dreams he is young again, he will recover from sickness. In general, dreams of youth are good.

ZEBRA. A dream zebra is a warning that you will have intimate dealings with a person who is not what he appears to be.

DREAMS IN VERSE

A maid to dream of verdant groves,
She'll surely have the man she loves;
But if the groves are nipped with frost,
She'll be as sure in marriage cross't;
A peacock tells 'twill be her lot,
To have a fine man, and a cot.
To dream of lambs, or sheep astray,
Her sweetheart soon will run away.
To dream of letters, far or near,
She soon will from her sweetheart hear.
To dream of bad fruit, her sweetheart
A fair face has, but false at heart.
To dream her sweetheart's at church zealous,
If she has him, he will be jealous.
A maid to dream of cats, by strife
She'll lead but an unhappy life.
To dream her sweetheart will not treat her,
'Tis well, if she has him, he don't beat her.
To dream her sweetheart gives a kiss,
Instead of blows she will have bliss.
If she dreams of bees, or honey,
When wife, he'll let her keep the money
And be mistress of his riches—
Nay, if she will, may wear the breeches;
And sometimes, life is not the worse,
Where gray mare is the better horse.
To keep things right in stormy weather,
Thong and buckle, both together.
To dream of timber, she'll be wed,
To one who'll be a log in bed;
But she'll be wed, who dreams of flies,
To one that will be otherwise.

BOOK II

THE BOOK OF FATE—ANSWERS TO QUESTIONS CONCERNING FUTURE EVENTS: DIVINATION THROUGH NUMEROLOGY.

On the following page you will find a list of thirty-five questions relating to the future. These are the questions most commonly asked astrologers and fortune tellers.

Here's what you do to get the answers.

Write four lines of words on a piece of paper. The lines should have a bearing on the question you wish answered and may even include the question itself. You may write your own full name for one line; the month, day and year for another; the name of a subject or person involved in the question for the third line, and so on. The lines do not have to be long. The question may even be broken up to form two lines.

When the lines are completed, count the letters (and numerals, if any) in each. If the total is an odd number, put a single dot (*) at the end. If the total is an even number, put a double dot (**) at the end.

Now turn to the key on page 47 and find the column containing the same series of dots as your four lines. Run your finger down the column until it is opposite the key number for the question you wish answered. The letter on which your finger stops, in the horizontal column following the question number, is your index letter. Find this letter on the following pages and again match your series of dots with the dots under the letter.

Your answer will be found where the dots and letters coincide.

QUESTIONS WHICH MAY BE ASKED

25.—Can I rely upon ——'s (naming the person) promises?
31.—Shall I acquire much property?
19.—Will she have a son or daughter?
29.—What does my dream signify?
17.—What sort of husband is ordained for me?
23.—Shall I obtain what I wish for?
27.—Will I win my lawsuit?
31.—Shall I make anything by this speculation?
15.—What sort of a wife (if any) shall I marry?
21.—Shall I meet with good success in life?
25.—Will my friend be true to his word?
 1.—Have I any enemies?
29.—What will be my luck if I marry?
23.—Will I succeed in my desire?
27.—Will I be fortunate this year?
21.—Shall I live to be very old?
25.—May I expect favorable news?
13.—Will —— (naming the person) be released from prison?
 3.—Who has got my (lost or stolen) property?
31.—Shall I ever inherit much property?
23.—Shall I prosper in what I now undertake?
25.—Is —— (naming the person) honest and candid?
11.—Is my lover sincerely true and constant?
29.—What will be my success in business?
 9.—Is my sweetheart honest and true to me?
21.—Shall I ever be married?
31.—Will my business yield much this year?
23.—Will this bargain be in my favor?
27.—Shall I recover my property?
 5.—How many children (if any) shall I have?
25.—Shall I marry the person I wish to?
29.—What will be my destiny?
 7.—Will the patient recover from illness?
21.—Shall I live happily in the married state?
27.—Shall I overcome my enemies?

KEY TO THE BOOK OF FATE.

Question | ** * * ** ** ** ** ** ** * * ** * * * * **

Question	**	*	*	*	**	**	**	**	**	**	*	*	**	*	*	*	*	**
	*	*	**	*	**	**	**	*	**	*	*	*	**	**	*	**	**
	**	*	*	*	**	**	*	*	*	**	*	**	**	*	**	*	**
	*	*	*	**	*	**	**	*	*	**	**	**	**	*	*	**	**

1	N	P	R	S	T	V	W	Z	L	K	H	G	F	B	C	D
3	L	K	H	G	F	D	C	B	N	P	R	S	T	V	W	Z
5	Z	W	V	T	S	R	P	N	B	C	D	F	G	H	K	L
7	B	C	D	P	G	H	K	L	Z	W	V	T	S	R	F	N
9	F	D	C	B	K	W	V	T	S	R	P	N	L	Z	G	H
11	T	V	W	Z	B	C	D	F	G	H	K	L	N	P	R	S
13	S	R	P	N	L	K	H	G	F	D	C	B	Z	W	V	T
15	G	H	K	L	N	P	R	S	T	V	W	Z	B	C	D	F
17	W	Z	T	V	R	S	N	P	K	L	G	H	D	F	B	C
19	C	B	F	D	H	G	L	K	P	N	S	W	V	T	Z	R
21	D	F	B	W	C	Z	G	H	R	T	L	V	K	N	S	P
23	H	L	G	R	D	T	S	C	V	F	Z	P	W	K	N	B
25	K	G	S	H	Z	N	F	D	W	B	T	R	C	L	P	V
27	P	N	L	K	V	F	Z	R	C	G	B	D	H	S	T	W
29	R	T	Z	F	W	L	B	V	D	S	N	C	P	G	H	K
31	V	S	N	C	P	B	T	W	H	Z	F	K	R	D	L	G

✸
✸ Only one living one—a
✸✸ daughter.
✸✸

✸✸
✸ Partially—but will be
✸✸ short lived.
✸

✸
✸ Possibly so, but somewhat
✸ doubtful.
✸✸

✸
✸ A fine boy.
✸
✸

✸✸
✸ The chances are favor-
✸✸ able.
✸✸

✸
✸✸ It is quite probable.
✸
✸

✸
✸✸ Yes, after a long time.
✸✸
✸✸

✸✸
✸ She is an angel.
✸
✸✸

✸
✸✸ A fidgety old maid of 36,
✸✸ but very loving.
✸

✸✸
✸✸ He is a gay deceiver; but
✸✸ he truly loves you.
✸

✸
✸ Two or three, who can-
✸✸ not injure you.
✸

✸✸
✸✸ Probably a large amount.
✸
✸✸

✸
✸✸ A young and handsome
✸ rich fellow.
✸✸

✸✸
✸ Good fortune.
✸
✸

✸✸
✸✸ Be assured the chances
✸✸ are favorable.
✸✸

✸✸
✸✸ A pretty, but very haugh-
✸ ty Miss.
✸

A young girl; you will probably suspect who she is but don't expose her as she may return it and be very sorry.

Some; but less than most people.

There can be nothing more sure.

A minister, who will be distinguished.

It is but barely possible.

Not for some time to come.

He merely wants a wife to shine his shoes and wait upon him.

A widow, with nine small children, and one at the breast.

She is heavenly true.

A large number, possibly twenty or more.

It is very uncertain.

An immense sum.

A black-eyed boy.

You may be sure of it.

Bad luck, unless you are wary.

The chances, at present, are excellent.

A flirt, who will run away from you.

Yes, you will.

You have very few real friends—and no decided enemies.

How can you have a doubt?

Not so much as you expect.

Yes—but with great difficulty.

A barber, disguised as a gentleman.

A sickly daughter.

It is quite probable.

It is very uncertain.

You will never have children.

A married woman has it now.

Parole from prison is sure.

He thinks you have money.

Fortune will attend you.

Without doubt.

C

A beautiful boy.

A preacher of excellent parts.

Happily and speedily.

You think well of a person who speaks ill of you.

Foolish man—she is too good for you.

An heiress of great beauty and accomplishments.

Yes, considerable.

All right, yes.

The chances are favorable.

Much prosperity.

He is weak and fickle, but you have his heart.

Fate wills it otherwise.

It has been sold, and you will stand little chance of getting it.

One every fifteen months —number uncertain.

You will realize all your expectations.

You will not.

51

G

✿✿ ✿ ✿✿ A big, husky man who will keep it in spite of you.	✿ ✿✿ ✿✿ There are several who hate you cordially.
✿ ✿✿ ✿ By no means.	✿ ✿✿ ✿✿ A devoutly pious man, but remarkably silly.
✿ ✿ ✿ Never.	✿ ✿ ✿ Yes.
✿✿ ✿ ✿✿ ✿ One who is lovely and amiable.	✿ ✿✿ As the fixed stars in the heavens.
✿✿ ✿✿ ✿ ✿ It is quite improbable.	✿ ✿✿ ✿✿ ✿ Seven healthy sons—one of which will be very distinguished.
✿✿ ✿ ✿ ✿ Don't calculate upon it.	✿ ✿ ✿✿ ✿ Good luck, and nine small children.
✿✿ ✿✿ ✿ ✿✿ A fine healthy daughter.	✿ ✿✿ ✿ ✿✿ You must be stupid, if you think otherwise.
✿✿ ✿✿ ✿✿ ✿ I fear not—but it is quite possible.	✿✿ ✿✿ ✿✿ ✿✿ Yes, but with considerable difficulty.

** You do her injustice by even a doubt upon the subject.

* It is quite doubtful if you have any.

* Yes, but you will have after troubles.

** You will be greatly favored.

** You may not.

** Don't worry—freedom is near.

* I am afraid not—watch your step.

** You may count upon it.

** You are not without enemies—but it is no fault of yours.

** A boy, who will be a great man.

* More than you anticipate.

* Yes.

** A gay deceiver, who has plenty of money.

* A very young girl, who will prove a scold.

** You must not expect it.

** A tall, slim, shabbily dressed man—he is very poor, and needs it more than you do.

*
** Three fine daughters.
*
**

* A little dumpy woman,
* with sharp black eyes—
* you will not be able to
* get it again.

** Unhappily, you will be
** very unfortunate.
**
**

**
* It is uncertain now—try
** tomorrow.
*

---

* That will depend upon
** your own prudence.
**
*

**
* Yes—but with trouble.
**

---

*
* There is no doubt of it.
**
*

* A blushing and red-
** haired maiden, remark-
* ably modest; too much
* so to escape suspicion.

**
* He is merely proud of
** your beauty.
**

**
** Not for a long time.
*
**

---

*
** Some—but less than you
** hope for.
**

**
** How can you ask such a
** silly question?
*

---

*
* A widower, with nine lit-
** tle children.
**

**
** A girl of extraordinary
* beauty
*

A very easy, good-natured
* person rather excites
* contempt than hatred
* —there are those who
** do not esteem you as
you deserve.

**
* The case is very danger-
* ous — prepare for the
* worst.

L

* One who has a good position and lots of money.

* Yes.

* You "love your enemy"— the only one you have —solve this.

* A cunning rogue, who will never return it.

* Yes, you will have good luck in that respect.

* Yes—after much suffering.

* Two only—a son and a daughter.

* A boy.

* As heaven itself.

* One pious, devoted and affectionate.

* If you avoid one accident, yes.

* No, you are not prompt enough.

* Don't be too sure, but I think so.

* Escape in this instance is certain.

* She is faithful and devoted to you.

* You will gain a great deal of property.

55

* ** Very doubtful indeed.

** * A fine gentleman, without cash.

* You stand a good chance.

** Most certainly.

** I am afraid he is not honest.

** You will never marry— being too diffident.

** More so than you are to her.

** It will be a long time first.

** You will be poor as a rat.

** It is very doubtful.

* A daughter.

* With great exertion, you may.

* A strange woman—you will see her yourself within two weeks.

** Evil reports against you have been circulated by persons beneath your notice.

** Do not borrow trouble— will yet be well.

** Five sons, all of them very smart.

** Pure as the freshly-fallen snow—and true as the fixed stars of space.	* One only—and he seems your friend.
** Riches and honor.	** It is very doubtful.
** I think so, but can't be positive today.	** A good-natured, good-looking, sluttish person, who delights in gay company.
** A promising son—but be careful of him.	** A shoemaker—but he will turn politician afterward.
** You will have more than you want.	** It has been taken off a great distance by two men—and hidden.
** You must not expect it.	** Yes, it is so ordained.
** There will soon be cause to rejoice.	** Don't worry; he's all right.
** It's very doubtful—you are too lazy.	** It is very doubtful indeed.

* ** I doubt it now—try again tomorrow.

* Yes—as speedily as the law allows.

* A neighbor—it is not 80 yards from you now.

* Vast wealth.

* Don't doubt it.

* You are unfortunate in this respect.

* The fates have ordained otherwise.

* The fates will it otherwise.

* A most interesting girl—but sickly.

* A rusty and crusty old bachelor.

* Consult this book tomorrow, using another four lines.

* You certainly will have none in wedlock.

* He is nothing else.

* You may, possibly—ask two days hence.

* Yes—you will be remarkably fortunate.

* A shrew; but smart, pretty and kind-hearted.

Being truly a very good-natured person, no one disputes the fact.	You will live in splendor and plenty.
Twin daughters and two sons.	You should have your head examined if you doubt her.
A little, good-natured fat fellow, who will get lots of money.	He only admires you—be cautious.
There is nothing in the world surer.	You may be sure.
You are too bashful to pop the question.	The fates are against you.
With proper caution, the case will terminate favorably.	That depends upon one circumstance.
You have a false friend, who knows where it is.	There can be nothing more certain.
A lovely daughter.	Not at present—but perhaps eventually.

Bad luck this time.

A fine boy.

Yes, with prudence.

That depends upon one act of yours.

It is quite uncertain—you may, perhaps, learn to-morrow.

Don't borrow trouble; freedom will come soon.

Positively, No.

You excite much gossip, but have no real enemies.

One who will deceive you.

An only son, who will die young.

She is somewhat coquettish, but she loves you truly.

A tall, light-complexioned man, but not very smart.

There is no need to apprehend danger.

You will have poor success.

A middle-sized, light-complexioned man, with red hair—unless you have remarkable luck you will never recover it.

As the sun.

V

Yes; in a very short time.

It is very uncertain—above a dozen, however.

If you are temperate and industrious, yes.

Young but rich.

A son, but sickly.

Yes, indeed; she never had an impure thought.

A female you little think would keep it—but she will.

It is uncertain now—next week you may learn.

Yes, with the exercise of common prudence.

Be careful—there are those who envy and watch you closely.

Do not doubt.

Yes, if you yourself are honest.

There are many chances in favor of it.

Yes, go ahead with confidence.

Doubt him not.

A very pretty girl but extravagant and coquettish.

W

A fine woman, but older than you.	You will be rich and respected.
That depends upon your habits.	A handsome man with black hair.
No, but do not despair, for you will be happy.	Four children, three of them girls.
The doctor knows it to be otherwise.	A daughter.
He's a wolf, but he's crazy about you.	No.
You stand in danger of an enemy—be careful.	You may be certain of it.
You may depend on it.	A young man whom you have seen, and have partial knowledge of.
You deserve your walking paper for asking that.	You will.

✿✿
✿✿ No, indeed.
✿✿
✿

✿✿
✿ He worships you.
✿
✿✿

✿
✿✿ A daughter of great
✿   promise.
✿✿

✿✿
✿ Yes, you'll be lucky.
✿
✿

✿
✿✿ Probably not for a con-
✿✿   siderable time.
✿

✿✿
✿✿ A most ingenious fellow
✿✿   —you will not get it
✿✿   again.

✿
✿ Yes, impudence.
✿✿
✿

✿
✿ There is little doubt of it.
✿✿
✿✿

✿✿
✿✿ Yes, but with some trou-
✿   ble.
✿✿

✿
✿ A very small amount.
✿
✿✿

✿✿
✿ Six—four sons and two
✿✿   daughters.
✿

✿✿
✿✿ None whatever.
✿
✿

✿
✿✿ You will meet with great
✿   difficulties.
✿

✿✿
✿ Most probably.
✿✿
✿✿

✿
✿ You will die an old maid.
✿
✿

✿
✿✿ A lovely girl from a
✿✿   wealthy family.
✿✿

BOOK III

GUIDE TO DREAMS AND LUCKY NUMBERS

Dream analysts, astrologers and numerologists have prepared extremely complicated tables defining dreams in terms of numbers which can be applied to the dreamer.

The following list is a simplified digest of these tables. Use it as soon as you can after dreaming. If you can recall your dream, you will probably find some object from that dream listed here. The numerals that correspond to the dream object are your lucky numbers for the day immediately following the dream.

TO DREAM OF AN

A-Bomb, is	72	Alabaster	7
Absence	4, 11	Alley	11, 17
Abyss	32	Almonds	61, 76
Accounts	7	Almsgiving	70
Acorn	7, 33	Altar	36, 51, 57, 62
Acquaintance	46	Ambassador	63
Acquisition	2, 19, 46	Amusement	48
Activity	10, 11, 75	Anchor	39, 58
Actress	14, 36, 52	Anchovy	57
Address	34	Andiron	28, 34
Adoption	21	Angel	14, 65
Adoration	24	Axe	7
Admiration	59, 71	Anger	41
Adultery	1, 11, 39	Answer	32
Adultress	69	Ant-hill	18
Affliction	3	Ants	2, 7, 41
Afternoon	13, 22, 65	Ape	4, 5, 6, 31
Air	42	Apparel	4, 13

69

71

72

75

LUNAR PROGNOSTICATIONS; LUCKY AND UNLUCKY DAYS; LOVE CHARMS AND SIGNS BY WHICH TO CHOOSE A MATE.

Part One

The Stages of the Moon As They Affect Newborn Children and Future Events

1. A child born during the new moon, or within twenty-four hours of a new moon, will be fortunate and live to a ripe old age.

2. The second day of the new moon is good for discovering lost articles; children born on this day will prosper.

3. The child born on the third day will become acquainted with important people who will help him in his endeavors.

4. The fourth day is bad; persons falling sick on this day rarely recover; children born on this day will be weak and sickly.

5. The fifth day is favorable for starting a new project; children born this day will be vain, selfish and deceitful.

6. Babies born on the sixth day probably will have a short life span, in most cases not exceeding 50 years.

7. On the seventh day, do not tell your dreams, for much depends on concealing them from others; the child born this day will live long but have many troubles.

8. Babies born this day will rise to a higher position than their parents.

9. The ninth day is about the same as the eighth; children born this day will attain wealth and personal honors.

10. Persons who fall ill on the tenth day will rarely recover, but children born this day will live long and be great travelers.

11. The child born this day will have a pleasing personality, good manners and a devout nature.

12. Children of the twelfth day will live long despite hardships.

13. Those born on the thirteenth day will be lucky, but quick profits will slip through their fingers.

14. If you ask a favor of anyone on the fourteenth day, it probably will be granted. Children born this day will be trusting and generous.

15. Babies born on the fifteenth day will become hard-working but frustrated adults.

16. This is a good day for buying and selling merchandise, but children born on the sixteenth day will be bad-mannered and unfortunate.

17. The child born on the seventeenth day will be foolish.

18. A child of the eigtheenth day will be courageous and will suffer considerable hardships.

19. The nineteenth day is dangerous, producing ill-tempered, malicious children.

20. A child born on the twentieth day will be dishonest unless strictly supervised in the early years.

21. Children born this day will be healthy, strong, selfish and self-centered.

22. The child of the twenty-second day will be cheerful and friendly.

23. The child born on the twenty-third day will have a terrible temper, will forsake his friends and choose to wander about in a foreign country, and will be very unhappy.

24. Children born on the twenty-fourth day will be greatly admired for extraordinary abilities and achievements.

25. The child of the twenty-fifth day will be sly, corrupt and deceitful; he will meet many dangers and may come to a bad end.

26. A child born this day will be rich and respected.

27. The twenty-seventh day is very auspicious for dreams and the child then born will have a pleasant disposition.

28. The child born on the twenty-eighth day will delight his parents but will not live to any great age.

29. Children of the twenty-ninth day will experience many hardships but will overcome them and eventually prosper.

30. The child born on the thirtieth day will be skilled in arts and sciences.

Part Two

Birth Days and the Future

SUNDAY. The child born on Sunday will live long.

MONDAY. A Monday child will be weak and effeminate.

TUESDAY. A vigorous nature and prone to violence.

WEDNESDAY. A child born this day will be intelligent, studious.

THURSDAY. The child shall achieve respect and a high position.

FRIDAY. A Friday child will be physically powerful and perhaps very lecherous.

SATURDAY. Most children born this day are of a dull, sluggish but determined disposition.

Part Three

Good and Bad Days TO BE Sick

1. For those who fall sick on the first day of any month, the third day of the illness is the time to watch out. Once this day is safely past, the patient will quickly recover.

2. An illness starting on the second day may be a long one, but the patient will recover.

3. Sickness on the third day won't last long.

4. Those falling sick on the fourth day may be ill for two weeks.

5. The illness that starts on the fifth day may be serious.

6. Those who fall ill this day probably will recover soon.

7. This is a lucky day. If you fall ill, you will quickly get well.

8. Sickness commencing on this day will be serious or even fatal.

9. Another unlucky day, denoting serious illness.

10. A sickness starting this day will be short and slight.

11. Same as the tenth day.

12. It is a bad omen to fall sick on the twelfth day of any month.

13. Those falling sick on the thirteenth day probably will recover.

14. Persons taken sick this day should recover within forty-eight hours.

15. Long illness, possibly fatal.

16. A sickness starting this day may be serious but is not usually fatal.

17. If a serious illness starts this day, the patient will die.

18. Those falling sick this lucky day will soon be well again.

19. Another fortunate day.

20. An uncertain day. If a serious illness starts, it could be fatal.

21. If the patient does not die within ten days, he will recover.

22. A sickness starting on the twenty-second day can be very serious. If the patient does not die in forty-eight hours, he will recover.

23. Lingering illness, then return to full health.

24. Serious sickness, partial recovery, then death within three months.

25. If you have to get sick, try to pick this day. Those falling ill on the twenty-fifth will recover quickly.

26. A lingering illness which starts on the twenty-sixth will end well.

27. Serious sickness, fifty-fifty chance of recovery.

28. Those who fall ill on the twenty-eighth may not recover.

29. Persons taken sick on the twenty-ninth will have a slow recovery.

30. Both the thirtieth and thirty-first are uncertain day and persons falling sick on either of them should not resume normal activities until their doctors pronounce them completely cured.

Part Four

Love Charms

The following charms and signs are recommended for unmarried girls who want to know who their husbands will be:

1. Feast of St. Agnes. January 21 is the day traditionally set aside in memory of St. Agnes, the virgin martyr. You must prepare yourself for a twenty-four hour fast, from midnight, January 20, to the following midnight. Take nothing but water in this period. Go to bed, sleep alone and do not tell anyone what you are doing. Lie on your left side and repeat these lines three times:

> St. Agnes, be a friend to me;
> Grant this that I ask of thee:
> Let me this night my husband see.

You will then dream of your future spouse. If more than one man appears, you will be married more than once. If you have no dream, you will never marry.

2. Wedding Cake. A thin slice of wedding cake, drawn three times through the bride's wedding ring, should be placed under the pillow of an unmarried woman. Then she will dream of her future husband.

3. Stocking sign. Before retiring, the girl should remove her right stocking and tie it to her left garter or the left fastener of her garter belt. Fasten them with seven knots and place under pillow. The girl will dream of her future husband.

4. Lenten charm. To be tried on any Friday during Lent except Good Friday. Take thirty-six blank cards or pieces of cards; write a different letter of the alphabet on each of twelve cards, write a different number on each of twelve additional cards; leave the remaining twelve cards blank. Now mix the cards or pieces, shake them in a box and draw one out. A letter signifies a happy marriage; a number, romantic intrigue; a blank card, no marriage in the near future.

Part Five

How to Choose a Mate

A ruddy complexion indicates a man or woman is healthy and good natured. A neat appearance signifies good breeding, personal pride and a generous nature. If the person you are considering has a lean, dark face that is often sad or frowning, you would not be happy with this one. A round-faced, broad-chinned man and a lively, dimple-chinned woman are a good match. If you are worried because your sweetheart's disposition is the opposite of yours, forget your fears. Opposites not only attract but fit well together.

BOOK V

NAMES AND THEIR LUCKY NUMBERS

"To dream of persons' names signifies a free conscience and a long life."

FEMALE NAMES AND THEIR NUMBERS

Adele	18, 21, 65	Corinne	25, 55, 76
Agnes	6, 7, 8	Darlene	2, 25, 70
Alexandra	17, 45, 78	Deborah	29, 47, 55
Alice	9, 16, 42	Diana	8, 13, 20
Alma	4, 13, 50	Dolores	6, 40, 60
Amelia	6, 9, 14	Donna	1, 18, 51
Amy	4, 8, 54	Dorothy	11, 12, 16
Anita	1, 8, 16	Edith	6, 8, 12
Ann, Anne	3, 7, 2, 49	Edna	22, 28, 63
April	9, 42, 30	Eileen	1, 7, 10
Arlene	14, 19, 20	Elaine	18, 56, 65
Audrey	27, 32, 40	Eleanor	5, 8, 61
Barbara	18, 42, 21	Elizabeth	5, 41, 56
Beatrice	17, 31, 45	Ellen	36, 62, 66
Betty	4, 14, 18	Elsa	51, 54, 74
Blanche	2, 7, 9	Emily	11, 16, 77
Bonnie	11, 42, 69	Estelle	9, 60, 70
Brenda	8, 19, 23	Eve	28, 41, 71
Brigitte	11, 17, 20	Faith	6, 17, 33
Candace	58, 62, 70	Felice	18, 44, 50
Carol	16, 22, 40	Frances	8, 17, 72
Catherine	42, 53, 64	Gail	19, 66, 69
Cecilia	11, 19, 40	Georgia	3, 46, 60
Charlotte	17, 35, 42	Gloria	18, 28, 75
Cheryl	4, 17, 20	Hannah	21, 46, 52
Christine	2, 8, 16	Harriett	21, 46, 60
Cindy	12, 17, 37	Helen	1, 21, 65
Clara	2, 8, 16	Hilda	2, 63, 69
Claudia	13, 36, 42	Holly	17, 19, 63
Constance	1, 60, 70	Ida	4, 11, 19

Irene	50, 71, 75	Norma	2, 3, 13, 21
Jacqueline	5, 10, 15	Olivia	12, 21, 42
Janet	2, 6, 17	Opal	38, 51, 66
Jean	7, 10, 11	Pamela	9, 11, 66
Jennifer	3, 6, 9	Patricia	2, 7, 9
Joan	2, 39, 53	Pearl	8, 19, 71
Joyce	11, 13, 56	Peggy	2, 19, 27
Judith	11, 56, 60	Penelope	3, 9, 40
Laura	11, 23, 38	Phyllis	8, 21, 42
Lena	1, 4, 7	Polly	4, 26, 54
Lenore	10, 16, 44	Rachel	2, 20, 22
Lillian	2, 5, 9	Rebecca	45, 73, 78
Lois	15, 68, 75	Regina	14, 27, 33
Loretta	5, 30, 40	Roberta	6, 60, 70
Louise	9, 19, 60	Rosalie	1, 54, 71
Madeline	4, 15, 18	Rosemary	15, 50, 51
Marcia	15, 69, 74	Ruby	29, 58, 67
Margaret	11, 21, 37	Ruth	18, 42, 65
Marianne	19, 23, 57	Sandra	2, 10, 56
Marilyn	31, 50, 78	Sarah	11, 19, 23
Marlene	30, 50, 56	Sheila	6, 14, 32
Mary	1, 20, 66	Shelley	33, 56, 60
Maureen	1, 18, 37, 40	Susan	6, 9, 54
Melissa	6, 9, 14	Thelma	8, 12, 42
Monica	3, 22, 44	Theresa	18, 22, 40
Myrna	18, 19, 20	Valerie	18, 27, 32
Nadine	7, 12, 69	Victoria	4, 13, 49
Nancy	8, 19, 27	Virginia	26, 36, 46
Natalie	4, 8, 11, 22	Wendy	19, 38, 91

MALE NAMES AND THEIR NUMBERS

Aaron	2, 67, 76	Archie	8, 20, 72
Abraham	13, 47, 74	Arne	1, 14, 36
Adam	12, 17, 48	Arnold	3, 16, 71
Adolph	28, 34, 62	Arthur	4, 33, 43
Albert	1, 10, 56, 60	Aubrey	16, 21, 47
Alexander	11, 22, 33	August	19, 36, 49
Alfred	17, 19, 21, 22	Barry	31, 51, 55
Allen	1, 11, 17	Bart	5, 14, 16
Amos	8, 24, 60	Benjamin	48, 49, 52
Andrew	17, 22, 31	Bernard	15, 41, 62
Anthony	10, 13, 21	Brian	15, 18, 70

Peter	34, 51, 66	Stuart	3, 5, 40
Philip	47, 58, 59	Terence	1, 22, 34
Preston	7, 43, 53	Theodore	45, 52, 59
Ralph	27, 32, 59	Thomas	11, 59, 67
Randall	20, 46, 66	Timothy	5, 12, 73
Raymond	1, 2, 15	Toby	4, 19, 74
Reuben	8, 24, 49	Tony	9, 37, 43
Richard	31, 66, 78	Troy	4, 44, 69
Robert	18, 64, 76	Vance	9, 16, 73
Roger	1, 10, 24	Vernon	8, 16, 42
Rolf	28, 59, 71	Victor	29, 36, 70
Ronald	16, 50, 76	Vincent	7, 12, 45
Russell	22, 38, 72	Wade	17, 23, 30
Samuel	15, 38, 75	Walter	19, 20, 50
Scott	40, 42, 58	Ward	42, 55, 76
Sean	10, 35, 44	Warren	7, 10, 11
Seth	18, 45, 57	Wayne	16, 39, 75
Seymour	24, 27, 45	Wilbur	8, 14, 22
Stanley	24, 31, 50	William	5, 11, 28
Stephen	4, 38, 71	Willis	4, 22, 50

LETTERS

If letters of the alphabet appear in dreams this is a good omen. The following list gives the significance of each dream letter and its lucky numbers.

A—Ambition	1, 5, 40
B—Beauty	2, 8, 29
C—Charity to all	3, 9, 46
D—Dangerous companions	4, 8, 16
E—You must endeavor to become popular	5, 22, 25
F—Faithfulness in love	5, 9, 16
G—Gentility	9, 40, 57
H—Honesty	9, 47, 69
I—Augurs ill	5, 9, 17
J—Joy and gladness	7, 19, 57
K—Maliciousness	38, 46, 63
L—Love and honor	27, 38, 69
M—Mercy and truth	7, 16, 31
N—Integrity	27, 73, 72

O—Enterprise 19, 21, 56
P—Prepare for misfortune 3, 20, 28
Q—Quarrels 1, 12, 60
R—Ruin and disgrace 16, 28, 43
S—High standing in society 19, 38, 57
T—Truth and honor 60, 69, 75
U—Denotes that you are very useful 11, 14, 39
V—Vexation and crosses in love 10, 15, 44
W—Increase of riches 15, 26, 69
X—Shows a stubborn disposition 6, 13, 43
Y—Loss of friends 1, 8, 25
Z—Hasty news 3, 19, 27

THE MONTHS

To Dream of Each Month and What It Signifies.

JANUARY—Signifies long life 19, 55, 63
FEBRUARY—Denotes riches and honor 13, 16, 75
MARCH—Denotes thrift and happiness, and that
    you will rise in the world 7, 15, 20
APRIL—Is a sign of sickness in the family 4, 7, 20
MAY—Predicts ruin and desolation 2, 4, 6
JUNE—Signifies success in love matters 3, 6, 9
JULY—Foretells some secret of your own will get
    out 8, 16, 42
AUGUST—Is a sign of bankruptcy through care-
    lessness 6, 17, 41
SEPTEMBER—Foreshadows success in your
    business 5, 9, 40
OCTOBER—Foretells misfortune, and you will
    perhaps become poor 8, 42, 62
NOVEMBER—Signifies you will have troubles
    through life 7, 9, 63
DECEMBER—Signifies contentment 8, 16, 79

BOOK VI

GAMBLER'S GUIDE: DICE, CARDS, MEANING AND NUMBERS

DICE

"To dream you win at dice means secret enemies are out to ruin you" (3, 35, 66). Here is what the dice spots denote, followed by lucky numbers for each.

One—Treachery 3, 19, 38
Two—Riches 2, 4, 6
Three—A pleasing surprise 4, 8, 32
Four—A disagreeable one 9, 17, 62
Five—A stranger who will prove a friend 1, 9, 10
Six—Loss of property 4, 8, 40
Seven—Undeserved scandal 33, 55, 70
Eight—Merited reproach 11, 22, 33
Nine—A wedding 1, 5, 10
Ten—A christening, at which some important
    event will occur to you 12, 21, 40
Eleven—A death that concerns you 9, 29, 59
Twelve—Special Delivery letter 4, 32, 27

DOMINOES

To dream of dominoes signifies good works and principally
weddings; to a prisoner it denotes liberty
and freedom. 23, 33, 66.

To Dream of Each One and What They Denote, With the
Numbers Attached.

Double-six—Receiving a sum of money 44, 55, 66
Six-five—Going to a public amusement .... 18, 65, sides
Six-four—Law suits 14, 64, 72
Six-three—Ride in a bus, train or plane 28, 63, 72

Six-two—Present of clothing 62, 64, 65

Six-one—You will do a friendly deed 5, 15, 21

Six-blank—Guard against scandals or you will
suffer by your inattention 2, 7, 10

Double-five—A new address to your profit 23, 28, 40

Five-four—A fortunate speculation 56, 66, 75

Five-three—A visit from a superior 2, 10, 56

Five-two—A beach party 7, 18, 50

Five-one—A love intrigue 5, 28, 75

Five-blank—A funeral, not a relation 18, 52, 60

Double-four—Drinking at a distance 21, 38, 74

Four-three—A false alarm 3, 4, 43

Four-two—Beware of thieves or swindlers. Ladies,
take note, this means more than it says 2, 4, 42

Four-one—Trouble from creditors 1, 4, 41

Four-blank—Letter from an angry friend 4, 10, 40

Double-three—Sudden wedding, at which you
will be vexed 3, 30, 33

Three-two—Buy no lottery tickets, nor enter into
any game of chance, or you will lose 2, 3, 23

Three-one—A great discovery at hand 1, 3, 31

Three-blank—An illegitimate child 4, 30, 21

Double-two—Vexations from a jealous partner 2, 4, 22

Two-one—You will mortgage or pledge some
property soon 1, 2, 21

Double-one—You will find something to your
advantage 11, 22, 41

Double-blank—You will soon have trouble.   10 to 70 combination.

CARDS

To Dream of and What They Signify.

The Ace of Clubs—Great wealth, much prosperity
in life and tranquility of mind 18, 68, 75

The King of Clubs—Announces a man who is
humane, upright, affectionate and faithful in all
his engagements; he will be very happy himself,
and make everyone else so, if he can 42, 49, 54

The Queen of Diamonds—The woman will not be a good housewife; she will continue to be a flirt, fond of male company and not always virtuous 7, 22, 40

The Knave of Diamonds—However closely related, he will look more at his own interest than yours 4, 5, 50

The Ten of Diamonds—Promises a husband or a wife with great wealth and many children; the card next to it will tell the number of children; it also signifies a wallet full of money 10, 13, 31

The Nine of Diamonds—Declares that the person will be a roving disposition, never contented with his lot, and forever meeting with vexations and disappointments 9, 16, 61

The Eight of Diamonds—The person involved will swear never to get married; if marriage does come, it will be late in life, to a person whose disposition will cause trouble 8, 42, 55

The Seven of Diamonds—Shows that you will spend your happiest days in the country, where, if you remain, your happiness will be uninterrupted; but if you come to town, you will be tormented by the infidelity of your conjugal partner 7, 68, 69

The Six of Diamonds—Shows an early marriage and widowhood; but that your second marriage will make you worse off 2, 4, 6

The Five of Diamonds—Shows marriage to a mate who will perform the bedroom duties so well that several children will result 5, 20, 29

The Four of Diamonds—Shows the person you marry will be unfaithful 4, 8, 32

The Trey of Diamonds—Shows that you will be engaged in quarrels, lawsuits and domestic disagreements; your partner for life will have an ungovernable temper, fail in the performance of the nuptial duties and make you unhappy 3, 16, 56

The Deuce of Diamonds—Shows that your heart will be engaged in love at an early period; that your parents will not approve your choice; and if you marry without their consent, they will hardly forgive you 2, 6, 7

The Ace of Hearts—Signifies fun, parties, feasting and good humor; if the ace be attended by spades, it foretells quarreling and ill-temper; if by hearts, it shows cordiality and affection; if by diamonds, your feast will be from home; if by clubs, the occasion of the meeting will be upon some bargain or agreement; if your ace of hearts is in the neighborhood of face cards of both sexes, with clubs near it, it will be about a match making; if all the face cards are kings or knaves, or both, it will concern the buying or selling of some personal property; if all queens, it will regard conciliation between parties, and if queens and knaves, it will be about the reconciliation of a married couple 1, 65, 66

The King of Hearts—Shows a man of fair complexion, of an easy and good-natured disposition, but inclined to be passionate, and rash in his undertakings 3, 19, 70

The Queen of Hearts—Shows a woman of a very fair complexion, or of great beauty; her temper rather fiery, one who will not make an obedient wife, nor one who will be very happy in her own reflections 11, 22, 40

The Knave of Hearts—Is a person of no particular sex, but always the dearest friend of the consulting party, ever active and intruding, equally jealous of doing harm or good, as the whim of the moment strikes, passionate and hard to be reconciled, but always zealous in the cause of the consulting party, though prone to act according to their fancy, as they will be as industrious to prevent their schemes as to forward them, if they do not accord with their own ideas 8, 32, 50

 Great attention must be paid to the cards that stand next to the knave, as from them alone you can judge whether the person it represents will favor your inclination or not 4, 8, 44

The Ten of Hearts—A generally good sign; if it appears next to bad luck cards, it will lessen their impact; if its neighboring cards signify good fortune, it confirms their value 10, 21, 27

97

The Nine of Hearts—Promises wealth, position and high esteem; if cards that are unfavorable stand near it, you must look for disappointment and a reverse; if favorable cards follow these last at a small distance, expect to retrieve your losses 9, 59, 69

The Eight of Hearts—Points out a strong inclination to get intoxicated; this, if accompanied with unfavorable cards, will be attended with loss of property, decay of health and falling off friends; if by favorable cards, it indicates reformation and recovery from the bad consequence of the former 8, 56, 65

The Seven of Hearts—Shows the person to be of a fickle disposition, addicted to vice and incontinence 7, 22, 25

The Six of Hearts—Shows a generous, open and credulous disposition, easily imposed upon, and ever the dupe of flatterers, but the good-natured friend of the distressed. If this card comes before your king or queen, you will be the dupe; if after, you will have the better 6, 9, 73

The Five of Hearts—Shows an unsteady disposition, never attached to one object, and free from any violent passion or attachment 5, 12, 60

The Four of Hearts—Shows that the person will not be married until very late in life, because he is hard to please and expects too much of others 15, 23, 44

The Trey of Hearts—Shows that your own imprudence will greatly contribute to your experiencing the ill-will of others 29, 70, 75

The Deuce of Hearts—Shows that extraordinary success and good fortune will attend the person, though if unfavorable cards attend, this will be a long time delayed 2, 8, 40

The Ace of Spades—Indicates many love affairs, both good and bad 62, 65, 69

The King of Spades—Shows a man who is ambitious and will succeed with the help of an important person; but there may also be reverses 33, 60, 69

The Queen of Spades—Shows a person who will be corrupted by both sexes; great attempts will be made on her virtue and she will have relations with both men and women 9, 11, 36

The Knave of Spades—Shows a person who, although they have your welfare at heart, will be too indolent to pursue it with zeal, unless you take frequent opportunities of rousing their attention 7, 36, 63

The Ten of Spades—Indicates bad luck, though its influence will depend largely on the cards that accompany it 9, 45, 48

The Nine of Spades—Portends dangerous sickness 11, 46, 64

The Eight of Spades—Shows opposition from friends 64, 8, 42

The Seven of Spades—Shows the loss of a most valuable friend 51, 54, 74

The Six of Spades—Shows a very great uncertainty in business 17, 21, 29

The Five of Spades—Shows that you will meet with one very fond of you 52, 46, 64

The Four of Spades—Shows sudden sickness 7, 10, 20

The Trey of Spades—Shows that you will be unfortunate in marriage, that your partner will be unfaithful 13, 31, 37

The Deuce of Spades—Always signifies a coffin, but for whom depends entirely on the other cards 7, 47, 74

GOOD COMBINATIONS TO PLAY

1, 10, 11, 42, 69

1, 10, 42, 44, 69

6, 9, 10, 11, 17, 44, 71

6, 10, 11, 44, 71

39, 50, 61, 74

4, 49, 74, 76

10, 51, 61, 70, 74

1, 10, 61, 64, 66

44, 66, 68, 70, 75

5, 25, 55, 65

4, 14, 56, 60

2, 12, 24, 72, 75

11, 44, 66, 77

2, 3, 4, 50

8, 46, 50, 59

3, 45, 55, 60

3, 25, 45, 55

3, 25, 42, 55

1, 2, 16, 40, 44

12, 24, 48, 62, 63

17, 39, 47, 50

6, 14, 25, 33, 46

13, 16, 53, 72, 73

17, 30, 44, 73

30, 72, 73, 75

9, 15, 17, 47

39, 46, 50, 61

15, 27, 66, 68

32, 33, 77, 78

1, 6, 16, 61

100

First Throw.

Second Throw ↓ \ First Throw →	II	III	IV	V	VI	VII	VIII	IX	X	XI	XII
II.	46	0	1	0	62	0	28	0	57	0	14
III.	69	37	0	13	0	78	0	17	0	70	0
IV.	33	60	12	0	61	0	71	0	10	0	27
V.	0	21	02	32	0	72	0	77	0	54	0
VI.	47	0	52	31	56	0	9	0	39	0	4
VII.	25	58	0	36	7	49	0	16	0	59	0
VIII.	74	66	40	0	64	35	3	0	41	0	75
IX.	0	76	24	68	0	20	73	45	0	8	0
X.	19	0	48	50	28	0	30	15	63	0	11
XI.	29	42	0	34	52	43	0	51	5	55	0
XII.	0	65	44	0	6	22	67	0	18	23	26

Explanation.—Take two dice and throw; mark down the number of spots thrown; then throw again, and mark as before; look at the top line of the table and find the number of your first throw; then follow the line straight down until you find on the opposite side of the table the number corresponding to your second throw. For instance, the number of spots in your first throw equals 6, which you will find on the top line of the table, marked in roman numerals, VI, your second throw gives 4 spots, which will be found on the outside column, marked IV. Place your finger on the VI at the top of the table, and follow the line down until it brings you to the IV, on the opposite side of the column; you will thus get the number 61, which will be the lucky number. In this manner you will get as many lucky numbers as you wish to play.

Numbers for Dreams of the Months

January	15	July	17
February	11	August	8
March	45	September	61
April	1	October	78
May	73	November	62
June	22	December	12

———

Thanksgiving Day	10	New Year's Day	4
Fourth of July	65	Washington's Birthday	73

BOOK VII

HUMAN PHYSIOGNOMY—HOW TO JUDGE A PERSON'S CHARACTER BY FEATURES OF THE FACE AND FORM OF THE BODY.

Part One

Corporeal Physiognomy—Lavater's Analysis of the Various Parts of the Body—Different Temperaments and Their Relations to Physical Characteristics.

> "Her pure and eloquent blood
> Spoke in her cheeks, and so distinctly wrought,
> That one might almost say her body thought."

These words by John Donne (1573–1631) prove he had a poet's instinct for estimating character on the basis of facial and physical features. We all possess this instinct, in greater or lesser degree; though we are not always aware of it.

"We are all physiognomists by nature," said a student of this subtle and subconscious art, which also has been called the Language of Looks.

How often have you heard a person described as having "bedroom eyes," "mean eyes," "a sneaky look" or "an honest face"? All of us make such snap judgments based on outward appearances. And when we do, we are practicing physiognomy.

The first time we meet a stranger, we receive an instinctive impression of his mental or moral character. Sometimes these impressions are formed from such flimsy evidence as a glance, smile or frown. Yet they can be amazingly accurate.

Of course, many men and women have trained themselves to create a deceptive image. And the observer's own nature—trusting, suspicious, gullible or jaded—may influence his view of others. But an alert physiognomist usually can read the true character behind the false face.

"Physiognomy" is a compound Greek word meaning "the law of, or an index to, nature." The Oxford Universal Dictionary defines it as:

1. "The art of judging character and disposition from the features of the face or the form and lineaments of the body generally . . ."

2. "The foretelling of destiny from the features and lines of the face; the fortune so foretold . . ."

3. "The face, . . . viewed as an index to the mind and character; expression of face; also, the general cast of features, type of face . . ."

This science of judging the inner man by his outer appearance has been practiced since humans first became curious about their own feelings and emotions.

More than 5000 years ago, the rulers of Mesopotamia and Egypt consulted their court physiognomists before making any important appointments or decisions. Later, the Hebrew, Greek and Roman poets and philosophers studied the language of looks, which had a marked influence on their writings.

Shakespeare was a talented amateur physiognomist and many of his characters, including Hamlet and Lady Macbeth, mirror his skill in the art of personality analysis.

Two centuries after Shakespeare brought physiognomy to the Elizabethan stage, English writer George Borrow (1803–1879) offered this advice to his countrymen:

"Trust not a man's words if you please, or you may come to very erroneous conclusions; but at all times place implicit confidence in a man's countenance in which there is no deceit; and of necessity there can be none.

"If people would but look each other more in the face, we should have less cause to complain of the deception of the world; nothing so easy as physiognomy nor so useful."

Borrow was right. There is nothing so easy as judging a person's character by the way he or she looks. Yet this can also be an extremely complicated process. And unless the observer knows what to look for, his conclusions may be completely erroneous or only partially correct.

The father of modern physiognomy was Dr. Johann Kaspar Lavater (1743–1801), a famous Swiss theologian and mystic.

Realizing that first impressions can be misleading, Lavater set out to determine the extent to which physical characeristics could be used as guideposts to mental and moral character. He devoted the better part of his lifetime to this project, wrote several books on the subject and created worldwide interest which has lasted to this day.

A friendly critic had this to say of the character-probing clergyman and his findings: "He was a good man, an ornament to humanity, possessed of subtle, observing and discriminating faculties and of a wonderful eloquence which have afforded great notoriety to his voluminous writings and more authority than they philosophically merit. For, being but slightly acquainted with the principles of physiology, he was unable in many instances to impute the facts which his acute penetration observed to their natural causes. He was consequently led into some whimsical vagar-

105

ies, and his unbounded enthusiasm for the subject occasionally beclouded his reasonings."

Here are some excerpts (translated into modern English) from Lavater's Theory of Corporeal Physiognomy:

THE HEAD. A short, round head indicates the owner is forgetful and foolish; a long, hammer-shaped head denotes a cautious, wary and prudent nature; a hollowness in the front of the head signifies a shrewd, sneaky character; a big-headed person is often dull and stupid, while a small-headed person is frequently foolish. The best head is one "of middling bigness," implying common sense and a good wit. Pineapple-shaped heads are often found on arrogant, boastful extroverts.

THE FOREHEAD. Smooth foreheads are found on flatterers, whom Lavater likens to fawning dogs; big, wrinkled foreheads imply boldness and strong character, also found in square-forehead types. Lavater felt low foreheads were a sign of sorrow and passion, while high foreheads implied a liberal, easygoing disposition. He found little good in these other shapes and sizes: "An over-wrinkled forehead, to be unashamed, and if puffed-up in the temples, to be high-minded, ireful and of a rude wit; the forehead small, to be unable to learn, and applied to the sow; the forehead very big, to be slow-witted, and applied to the ox; the forehead round, to be of dull perseverance, ireful, and applied to the ass."

EYES. Small, quivering eyes indicate shyness and also passion. They are found on both bashful virgins and bold lovers. The bigger the eyes, the less malice

—and the more foolishness. Pop-eyed people tend to be foolish, fearful and faint-hearted. Shifty eyes indicate a rash, unruly and troubled nature; their owners can't be trusted. Quivering eyelids are a sign of fear. Sharp, fast-moving eyes indicate a person who, according to Lavater, is "fraudulent, unfaithful and a thief." But someone with steady eyes also may be "troubled in mind and a deceiver." Baggy eyes belong to heavy drinkers, puffy eyes to heavy sleepers. Hollow eyes denote envy and wickedness, though eyes only "somewhat hollow" imply great courage. Large, oxlike eyes signal a gentle, trusting disposition or simply stupidity. The eyes of malicious people sometimes have fleshy inner corners adjoining the nose, while those of crafty schemers are long and narrow. Big, trembling eyes mark a man "desirous of women."

NOSE. A round nose with a sharp end like a bird's bill indicates a wavering, unsure mind; crooked-nose types are arrogant and unstable; a nose curved like an eagle's beak is a sign of courage. A flat nose implies the owner is lecherous, bad-tempered or both. Large nostrils are worn by the honest and bold. A large, turned-up nose is a sign of greed. Sharp noses denote impatience and vicious tempers, while round, blunt noses imply quiet strength.

EARS. Envious, jealous people have long, narrow ears. Dull, sluggish dopes sport large ears, worn close to the skull. People with round ears have difficulty learning. Small ears denote rude, crude scoffers. But the proud possessors of "ears of a middling bigness" are faithful and generally honest. Hairy ears are the best of all, indicating good hearing and long life.

THE FACE. A small, sweaty face indicates a person who is "crafty, lecherous and a great feeder." A long, lean face implies the owner is bold, crooked and malicious. Most fools have little, round faces, while liars have long jaws. If the lower half of the face is narrow, expect an envious, quarrelsome disposition. Narrow faces also denote stinginess. Slow, cautious types usually have fleshy faces. Hollow cheeks go with cranky, quarrelsome people. And twisted faces may be the tip-off to twisted minds.

LIPS. Full lips indicate warmth and passion. A large upper lip, hanging over the lower, is the sign of a fool. But if the overhanging lip is thin, the owner probably is bold and rugged. Thin, tight lips go with people who are petty, mean, cheap and argumentative. Thin, soft lips show strength of character.

CHIN. Effeminate people, both male and female, usually have round chins. If a man has a hanging underchin, he is probably lecherous. A dimpled chin is the mark of a tricky, lustful person. Faithful friends may have sharp chins, but a chin both sharp and small means envy, jealousy, cruelty. According to Lavater, this is the sign of the serpent. The square-jawed chap is honest, industrious and strong.

BEARDS. Lavater regarded unkempt, untrimmed beards, like those worn by today's beatniks, as indicative of an evil nature. He also concluded that women with facial fuzz were lecherous.

TEETH. Wide teeth, a dull, lascivious nature; long, sharp teeth, a big appetite and a terrible temper.

VOICE. A small, soft, quavering voice signifies fear or uncertainty. But a soft, steady voice means a gentle nature. A loud, high-pitched voice implies a nervous, fretful disposition and a big, brassy voice usually belongs to a braggart who listens to no other sound but his own braying.

NECK. Most witty people have short necks. Big, strong necks are a sign of masculinity and thin, slender necks of effeminacy. Long, narrow necks also indicate a fearful nature.

BREASTS. If a man has a hairy chest, he is vigorous and virile. If he has fat, flabby breasts, he is weak and effeminate. A woman with full, firm breasts is kind, generous and sensuous. A woman with thin, hanging breasts is inclined to be nervous, irritable and spiteful. "Ptolemy writeth: The breast big and well-fashioned, to be strong; hairy on the breast, to be inconstant and bold."

SHOULDERS. Sharp shoulders denote a deceitful nature; broad shoulders, strength and good character; narrow shoulders indicate a dull, self-centered person; stoop shoulders imply weakness and laziness; well-built shoulders signal a healthy, liberal disposition, but if they are a bit too thin a tendency to stinginess is indicated.

STOMACH. Small, round belly, a good disposition; large, swollen belly, a glutton; much hair from the navel downward, a windbag, braggart or gossip; much fat above the stomach, a healthy appetite and great physical strength.

BACK. A crooked back implies a stingy, mean, insecure person. A narrow back implies moral, emotional or physical weakness. A large, well-formed back indicates strength and generally good character.

ARMS. "The arms hairy, to be inconstant and lecherous; the arms very long, to be strong, bold, honest and gentle; the arms short, to be a promoter of discord and lecherous."

HANDS. Small, fidgety hands denote an inconstant, crafty, untrustworthy nature; large hands indicate physical strength; short, wide hands imply a rude, dull person. Lavater also held that a person with broad hands and narrow fingers was likely to be a "rioter" in his youth, while one with fat fingers was likely to be a thief.

FINGERNAILS. Very short nails are the sign of an evil, unscrupulous nature; small, crooked nails imply greed; tiny nails also indicate a crafty, treacherous person, always alert to take advantage of others. White specks on the nails signify a fortunate person who will make a lot of money and friends; black specks indicate a capacity for making enemies. Long, smooth, thin, clear nails, white or pink in color, imply good health, good humor and a ready wit. Long, narrow, sharp nails denote a cruel, fierce disposition. Rough, round nails imply an oversexed person who, according to Lavater, is "prone to the venereal act."

TOES AND TOENAILS. Well-formed toes with thin, pink nails indicate a healthy, intelligent, well-balanced person; toes very close together denote a fearful, unsure disposition; crooked toes and nails imply a bold, brash character.

RIBS. "The ribs filled out, as if they were blown up, to be full of words and foolish; the person well-ribbed, to be strong; the ribs narrow and frail, to be weak."

HIPS. Muscular hips denote strength of body and character; fleshy hips indicate an indolent, fun-loving, sensual or effeminate nature; narrow hips imply weakness, nervousness.

LEGS. Slender legs imply an athletic, active, aggressive and perhaps nervous individual; large calves mean a sluggish, dull, rude-mannered person, but medium-sized calves denote intelligence and strength of character; brawny, muscular legs imply great physical strength; small, cordlike sinews indicate a lustful, libidinous nature; soft, smooth or flabby legs are a sign of effeminacy in men; crooked or bow legs imply a bold, aggressive character.

ANKLES. Broad, muscular ankles show strength; too thin or too fleshy ankles, weakness. Slender ankles also may indicate a fearful, erratic temperament.

FEET. "The feet thick and short, to be weak; the feet slender and short, to be wicked; the feet fleshy and hard, to be a blockhead; the feet small and fair-formed, to be a fornicator; the feet much hairy, to be lecherous and bold; the feet naked of hair, to be weak of strength and courage; the feet weak, sinewed and small, to be effeminate." Lavater also held that people with fleshy insteps were crafty and those with big, fat feet were fools.

HAIR. Hair on the back signifies a cruel, domineering type. Men with hairy chests, stomach, legs and shoulders are extremely virile, fickle and constantly seeking sexual gratification. Men with little or no body hair are effeminate and inclined to homosexuality. Excess body hair on women denotes passion.

WALK. If a person walks with the feet and knees turned in, he is weak and unsure of himself; if his stride is slow and long, he is intelligent and deliberate; if the stride is quick and long, he is strong yet inclined to be foolish; a short, quick pace indicates a weak, indecisive character. A stealthy, furtive walker usually is up to no good. A person who walks straight ahead, with his shoulders thrust slightly forward, is aggressive, self-assured and generally of good character.

POSTURE. The person who stands erect and looks others directly in the eye is self-assured and generally intelligent, though his motives may not be as clear as his posture indicates. The sloucher tends to be weak, nervous, unsure of himself. The woman who flaunts her physical attributes, deliberately creating an aura of sensuality, is often neurotic and sexually frigid.

While Lavater's deductions were not always correct, and in some cases bordered on the ridiculous, his studies aroused an enormous interest in physiognomy and opened the doors to modern research in this field.

To Lavater's findings were added the conclusions of the Austrian metaphysician Franz Joseph Gall. Around 1800, Gall developed the theory now known as phrenology or "head-bump analysis." Phrenologists maintain that different mental faculties are seated in separate parts of the brain and that the development of each faculty may be judged by the shape of the skull overlying its particular position.

Introduced to America by Orson and Lorenzo Fowler, phrenology quickly attracted nationwide interest. Modern researchers in the field of character analysis through physical traits use the basic principles of both physiognomy and phrenology in their work.

Corporeal physiognomy, therefore, is the antithesis of psychiatry and psychology. These latter sciences are concerned with the mind's influence over the body while corporeal physiognomy deals with the influence which the body has over the mind.

Serious students of physiognomy must gain a working knowledge of the human mind, the brain and all the component parts of the human anatomy. For the essence of corporeal physiognomy depends upon the relative development of the body parts in different individuals.

The study begins with the division of body organs and functions into three classifications—locomotive, vital and mental.

The first includes the bones, which are the mechanical instruments of motion; the muscles, which are the agents of motion, and the tendons and ligaments which join the bones and muscles.

The second class consists of tubes and vessels of various kinds, such as the absorbing, the secreting and the circulating blood vessels—in short, those organs which immediately nutrify and support the body.

The third comprises the sensory organs, the brain, and the network of nerves that connect them.

Now, the fundamental principle of corporeal physiognomy is that as one of the above three classes predominates in the human system, so will a tendency to its peculiar functions be manifested. From this predominance, we can judge a person's character or mental makeup, though not the peculiar functions of the mind.

Temperament—a person's nature or disposition—is the key to corporeal physiognomy. There are, of course, several species of temperament and all have been explained in detail by physicians, psychologists and philosophers. For our purposes, it will be necessary only to mention a few of the basic ones according to their physical classifications.

A person in whom the locomotive organs predominate is of the so-called muscular temperament. If this class of organs prevails over the others, the individual will have long, powerful limbs and probably will be more disposed to exercises of the body than of the mind. Strength and manly beauty are the main characteristics. The legendary Hercules, the Roman gladiators, professional athletes and most heroes of the movie and television screen belong to this class.

The vital organs produce two main species of temperament, based on the action of blood and lymphatic vessels. If the blood vessels prevail, a sanguine temperament emerges. If the lymphatic vessels are the determining factor, a phlegmatic temperament results. In both of these, but particularly in the latter, the legs and arms are shorter and the upper body fuller than in the muscular temperament. And there is either a greater or lesser tendency to corpulence.

The sanguine temperament implies a naturally cheerful, confident and hopeful disposition; also a passionate and sometimes fickle nature. The phlegmatic temperament is just the opposite—a sluggish, sturdy, indifferent type who prefers food, drink and sleep to physical, mental or sexual exercise. A perfect example of this temperament is a person of whom it is said "He never loses his cool."

In the last of the three classes, the mental organs and nerves predominate and produce a natural nervous temperament. Those who have it are inclined to be highly intelligent, sensitive, erratic and emotional, with rigid, diminutive bodies.

This is the temperament of genius. Nearly all great men who have moved the world with the strength of their intellect have belonged to this category of temperament.

Body conditions, such as "bilious" and "melancholic," have sometimes been classified as primary temperaments. However, these are merely mixtures of the basic temperaments, reflecting the struggle of competing body organs.

Occasionally the three classes of organs are so equally compounded that the resultant temperament is either neuter or indeterminate. But one system usually predominates and leaves its stamp on the temperament or character. However, one class rarely is so predominant that the temperament emerges with no trace of the subordinate classes. When this is the case, it is obviously unnatural. A rare, undiluted temperament may indicate a mental or nervous disorder.

In strongly marked cases, the temperament "grows with our growth and strengthens with our strength," but more often it is modified by external circumstances and the mode of life. Therefore, members of certain races and professions acquire similar temperaments.

The passionate Italian, the stolid German, the fiery Frenchman, the beefy policeman and the absent-minded professor are all classic examples of temperament-conditioning.

Temperament influences not only a person's looks, deeds and habits, but also his mental action.

Both the quality and activity of the brain are very much modified by the temperament. The brain is an organ, possessing a similar texture and subject to the same general laws as the other body organs. Hence, like the muscles and nerves, its fibers are denser and more rigid, and consequently possess most intensity of action, in the nervous temperament.

In the sanguine temperament, the brain is fed by larger blood vessels. There is somewhat less mental activity though a high level of excitability is maintained. In the phlegmatic temperament, there is a greater quantity of watery lymph in its cells. The brain is affected by the body's general flaccidity and it too becomes dull, inert and lethargic.

Numerous tests prove that the blood is the chief stimulus to the brain. The faster blood circulates through the brain, the more mental activity accelerates. If the supply of blood to the brain is suddenly cut off, the result is a mental blackout (fainting, a coma) followed by death.

A sluggish flow of blood to the brain creates a "sluggish mind." Conversely, a rising fever circulates the blood with increasing rapidity, stirring the brain to such frantic activity that it frequently spins into delirium.

Persons of sanguine temperament have particularly well-developed heart and blood vessels. Consequently, they are easily excited to powerful action. Flashes of brilliant but superficial wit, anger and unstable vehemence of feeling characterize this temperament.

Phlegmatic persons are almost entirely dependent on the glands and lymphatics, which are the chief organs for nourishing the body. Their lives are mainly vegetative. Most of their energies are expended in increasing their bulky frame and the little mental action they exhibit is feeble and slow.

John Wolcot, the eighteenth-century English poet who wrote under the name Peter Pindar, observed that "Fat holds ideas by the legs and wings."

And Shakespeare, a nervous temperament type himself, put these words in the mouth of another such, Julius Caesar:

"Let me have men about me that are fat,
Sleek-headed men, and such as sleep o' nights;
Yon Cassius has a lean and hungry look;
He thinks too much—such men are dangerous.
Would he were fatter."

Part Two

Emotive Physiognomy—Looks, Gestures and Postures of Different Dispositions

Corporeal physiognomy, briefly described in the preceding chapter, deals with the human body's influence on the mind. Emotive physiognomy concerns itself with the influence the mind exerts over the body.

Most people express their feelings with looks and gestures that eventually become habitual. From them, the trained observer can judge the mind which has produced them.

Gesture is the involuntary muscular movement triggered in the body by the passions of the mind. It undoubtedly preceded the spoken word. For this reason, it is sometimes called the natural language.

A person's posture, eye movements and walk also are part of this unspoken, unwritten language.

In walking the streets, the man who thinks of the future looks upward; the man who thinks of the past looks down. If he looks straight ahead, he is occupied with the present; if he looks right and left, he is thinking of nothing important. If he casts frequent looks behind him, he is probably thinking of his creditors.

The man who walks slowly is reflecting, meditating, calculating. The man who projects moves rapidly while he who runs is trying to catch up with success—in money, love or personal ambition.

The man who takes short, mincing steps, contracts his eyes, thrusts his face forward and twitches his shoulders is boastful, faultfinding, punctilious—and probably a cheat. If he rolls his body and jerks his arms, he is either a discotheque habitué or a politician.

The man who always wears the latest and sharpest fashions usually has little else to think about. He is petty-minded, irritable and a born sucker.

Clothes do not always make the man. But his clothes always indicate what type of man he is.

Laughter is another indication of character. As a chuckle-decoder once said: "The man who is always laughing is an idiot; the man who never laughs is a jackass; the false man seldom gets beyond a sneer. The hearty laugher is undoubtedly honest; the horse-laugher is a vulgar bore. Simperers invariably think themselves pretty. The man who laughs convulsively has a touch of madness."

The same physiognomst observed: "The busy man looks without seeing; the lazy man sees without looking; the lounger, a meditative man, both looks and sees without appearing to do either."

And the man who walks rapidly past a pretty girl without giving her even a sidelong glance—this man has problems, either domestic, business, financial or psychological.

From these few examples, the reader should get an idea of what emotive physiognomy is all about. Every gesture, glance and grimace has a meaning. By watching a person walk and talk, the trained observer can tell a great deal about his temperament, character and thought processes.

All humans are endowed with mental faculties that respond in various ways to external stimuli. Each of these faculties, when activated, makes itself known through some physical reaction. The emotions triggered by the sight of blood, for example, may make a person gasp, scream, faint or turn pale. Both tears and laughter are common physical responses to mental impressions.

Each emotion expresses itself through instinctive bodily action. This is its natural language. And there are as many different dialects as there are different faculties of the mind.

The mind so controls specific gestures that few people can be under the influence of any strong emotion without expressing it in their features or in unconscious physical responses. We cannot even imitate these responses without experiencing in a minor degree the corresponding mental feeling.

For this reason, actors cast in difficult dramatic roles experience all the mental turmoil of the characters they portray. Richard Burton and Elizabeth Taylor, who fell in love while playing the lovers Mark Antony and Cleopatra, came close to an emotional bustup while portraying a battling husband and wife in the movie "Who's Afraid of Virginia Woolf."

During filming, Burton disclosed: "The worst part is the domestic battle. I told Elizabeth, 'You've got to do it to prevent anyone else doing it.' But no matter how intelligent one is, the part rubs off.

"It's going to be a rough ride for us. And we may get rough with each other."

Because they are constantly cast in different parts requiring different emotional responses, actors provide a particularly fertile field for the study of emotive physiognomy. A veteran thespian once remarked: "Put on the wrinkled brow of anger, shoot out the curling lip of scorn or assume the dimpled cheek of joy and you will experience the appropriate feeling —and you cannot entertain another sentiment at the same time without betraying it in the gestures of some other part of the features."

French Count George Louis Leclerc de Buffon, a contemporary of Lavater, held that "all people who live miserably are ugly and ill made."

There have been many exception to this theory, the late Marilyn Monroe among them, but it is generally true that a person's background molds his mental reflexes and that these, in turn, are expressed in the physical appearance.

In his fiction classic "Oliver Twist," English author Charles Dickens wrote: "Alas! how few of Nature's faces there are to gladden us with their beauty. The cares and sorrows and hungerings of the world change them as they change hearts; and it is only when those passions sleep, or have lost their hold forever, that the troubled clouds pass off and leave heaven's surface clear."

But Dickens also observed: "I have known a vast quantity of nonsense talked about bad men not looking you in the face. Don't trust that conventional idea. Dishonesty will stare honesty out of countenance, any day in the week, if there is anything to be got by it."

Dickens was right in both instances. The dishonest man's frank, open stare is a conditioned reflex. And the serious student of physiognomy should be able to spot its true meaning just as easily as he reads the natural, instinctive responses to mental activity.

BOOK VIII

SIGNIFICANCE OF BIRTHMARKS

A mole or birthmark over the heart signifies an evil, deceitful or lascivious nature.

On the stomach, it is the sign of a glutton; on the bottom of the stomach, it indicates weakness or ill health.

If a man has a mole on the knee, he will have a pretty wife; if a woman has a birthmark on the right knee, she is honest and virtuous; on the left knee, she will have many children.

A mole on the nose signifies a restless person who will travel in many lands. A throat mole signifies wealth. A woman with a mole on the lower jaw will have trouble bearing children. A man with a birthmark on his tongue will marry a rich and famous woman.

A lip mole is the sign of a very amorous person.

If a man has a mole on his chin, he will attain a lot of money and possessions. A woman with a chin mole also will become wealthy. Moles on the ears and neck also foretell fortune.

A mole on the back of the neck signifies a serious accident which could be fatal. A birthmark on the loins signifies a weak person who will never be out of debt.

The lucky person with a mole on the throat will find a marriage partner who is both wealthy and good-looking. On the hand, a mole portends prosperity, good luck and enjoyment of children; on the breast, it means financial or romantic problems; on the left shoulder, it denotes troubles, affliction and, if near the arm, quarrels, strife and hatred.

A mole on the right forehead or temple signifies success in job or business; on the left cheek, it denotes poverty; on the left corner of the eyes, sadness and sorrow.

A birthmark on the right earlobe is a warning of death by drowning. A mole at the bottom of the nostrils is a lucky sign. The person with a mole on the right breast is ingenious and hard-working; the person with a mole on the left breast is unlucky in love.

A mole on the left cheek means poverty and sickness; on the right cheek, it means health and wealth. On the right foot, it signifies wisdom and eloquence; on the left foot, foolishness, rash actions and a habit of speaking before thinking.

Moles on the knuckles are good luck omens. So are moles on the toes.

A mole on the right side of the groin is a lucky sign, but bad luck accompanies a mole on the left side. A mole on the eyebrows indicates a happy marriage.

A mole on the right thigh indicates riches and better connections through matrimony. On a woman's right knee, it means a loving husband and easy childbirth.

In general, moles on the thighs, hips and loins imply a weakness of character that can lead to misfortune. A mole on the private parts signifies a passionate nature and a wide variety of love affairs.

BOOK IX

BIRTHDATES AND THEIR LUCKY NUMBERS

Each day of the month has a special significance for anyone born on it. In fact, there are two things that are important about each day. One is the meaning of that date in itself and the other is the Fadic number of each date and its importance relating to all things concerned with numbers, such as lucky days, betting, omens and such.

First, the meaning of each date. Whatever date you were born on, use the following explanations as your guide to life. Or look up the birthday of someone you know to find out things about them that they may not even know.

1. If you were born on the first day of the month, you were born to be one of life's leaders. You're a self-starter, an initiator, an innovator. And if you can't start out on top, you don't so much rise as force your way to the forefront. You expect to be heard and you expect to lead. The number 1 is symbolized by the sun. It represents creation, the beginning of all things. It doesn't receive. It gives.

So you will be positive, definite, creative, leading the way for others to follow. You don't look around to see if others will follow. You forge ahead on your own because as far as you're concerned the way you choose is the right way, the only way. Others sense this definiteness in your character and, lacking the same sureness, stand aside for your authority.

You dislike restraint and you tend to see others' authority over you as, at best, a temporary inconvenience. You command respect and your idea of friendship is other people respecting you. Even then, you would just as soon be left alone, though you do rather enjoy having others at your feet.

Whatever you do, you go your own way, and the rest of the world can take it or leave it.

You are strong, determined and generally good-natured in a grumpy sort of way.

2. This is the number of imagination, of dreams and of romance. You see beyond the here and now to the dreams of better, more beautiful worlds. You don't just see them. You believe in them and sometimes stake your life on your dreams. The only problem is that others don't always see them, certainly not so well as you do—even when you tell them.

Fortunately, even though most others don't understand you, you have the gift of understanding them. You have an almost uncanny sympathy for people's point of view, for you can almost always see the other side of every question. And you adapt, getting beyond the narrowness and shortsightedness that surrounds you to the magnanimity you believe all should have.

Unfortunately, this attitude doesn't always get you what you want. Rather, it helps others get what they want, while you keep dreaming. You can succeed, however, by using your wonderful diplomatic gifts if you can couple them with the singular determination to get practical rewards in the here and now by doing practical things.

3. You people born on the third of the month are ambitious and energetic. You are never happy unless there are commands to be given, orders to be followed and work to be done. You know that the work and the orders will lead you to the one spot you feel comfortable in—being in charge. You don't mind taking orders because you know it will lead you sooner or later to the position of giving them. You don't chafe under authority the way a 1 does. To you authority is in the natural order of things. Someone has to have it. And being at home

with orders and authority is one of the reasons you find it so easy to give orders—you just don't have any doubts about the rightness of your command.

Another reason is that you feel right at home being the judge of other people. There are probably more judges and generals born on the third than any other day.

You are also rather happy people. You don't like to go into things too deeply. You want to get things done and get on with it. That includes being unhappy. Find out what's wrong and take care of it is your attitude.

Your only real fault is that you tend to overdo all these things. Your judgments are fair but they can be too hard. There's usually nothing wrong with your commands but you tend to give them from "on high," as if no one else had a right to an opinion. And you tend to crash through other people's deeper problems because you're too impatient, insisting on good spirits to the point of insensitivity.

If you can cure yourself of these brash characteristics, or at least temper them a bit, you will find that your positive, commanding, good-natured manner will take you farther and faster than anything else you can do.

4. People born on the fourth mix many of the traits of the previous three numbers in a way that is all their own. Like the 1 people, you 4's are very content in your own view of things. In fact you are even more stubborn than a 1 is. Like the 2's, you see things from unusual angles most people wouldn't think of. But you are not dreamers, for like the 3's, you are very practical in your outlook. You are more down to earth than a 3, though. Hard work, application and particularly detail are second nature to you. You like to see tasks through to completion. On one hand, you like to see things finished, not left dangling. Get it done and get on to the next thing. And on the other hand, you like to make sure every detail of an operation is properly taken care of. You pride yourself on this and you feel that others aren't doing their job properly if they don't follow every facet through to the end.

Your attitudes toward work and detail are so strong that you tend to bury a lot of emotion deep inside you. It isn't that you aren't emotional. Underneath there is a free spirit that yearns to get out, but there are too many important things to get done, too much work to attend to. This is not such a bad attitude as many would think, because you get a lot of things done and that is a great source of satisfaction to you. You can point to your accomplishments and know that you haven't wasted your time.

You are, in fact, one of the cornerstones of society. You are one of the builders, the makers, the ones who get things done.

You tend to worry about your health, particularly the food you eat. You believe one should visit the doctor regularly and take care. After all, there's work to be done. You are very determined and usually—for all your worry—quite strong. If you could relax a little, just feel content to rest, you would still get a lot done, and feel a lot better.

5. People born on the fifth are the communicators, the mixers and the motivators. You have an almost magical power to communicate your ideas to other people, whether they want to listen or not. You may not always want to, for you are the most excitable of people. And once you've been set off, you don't really have any ideas, but you communicate your feelings anyway. And you usually carry the moment by sheer energy and will.

You tend not to think about the future except in the vaguest possible terms. You're completely wrapped up in the needs of the moment. Consequences are irrelevant, for you can deal with them when they get around to you, the way you deal with everything else—on the spur of the moment. Fortunately, you're real good at this. You don't even think it's very unusual.

You do find everyone else a bit slow on the uptake, however. They also seem a bit wishy-washy for your taste, sooner or later.

On the other hand, if you can control your temper and your somewhat sensual excitability, and turn your rapid-fire brain to ideas and method and particularly to tolerance, the things you can accomplish are phenomenal. But you'll probably get bored long before you see anything through to the end, if it takes more than one sitting.

You also hate restraint in even the mildest form. The only thing you are sure to work at for as long as it takes, is getting yourself free from whatever bit you think is in your mouth.

The compensation for all this difficulty is your flashing wit, high spirits, and invincible faith in your own point of view. No knock, however severe, leaves you daunted, or even dented. You may go crazy over the little stuff, but the really big setbacks that would crush everybody else leave you unconcerned, ready to tackle a new day.

6. Those of you born on the sixth are the hardheaded idealists of the world. You believe in following a code, you have high standards and you believe in honest work to accomplish things. With such an attitude it's not surprising you attract followers. People understand you are a person of high character and clear practicality. You expect to do business in a businesslike way. Many lawyers and merchants are born on the sixth.

You are also a person of considerable enterprise. It wouldn't occur to you to sit around and wait for fate to open the door for you. That's what handles are for. And you could be characterized as a person who spends most of your life getting the handle on things.

There is also a considerable magnetism about you. It isn't the noisy sort that some people have. It's the quiet, strong, clear magnetism of a person who knows how to get things straightened out and get them moving.

Though you are unyielding, you have a strong loving instinct. It is not the sensual, physical kind of love others are dependent on. Yours is more familial, the warm, trusting, ideal love that most others pretend to, but which you really mean. It isn't surprising you attract devoted followers.

7. The number of magic, 7, gives to those born on its day the ability to feel the forces around them, the meaning and the power of nature, the feelings and even the truth of those around them. You have an uncanny insight into the problems of others, which you usually do not even appreciate yourself. You don't notice what is plain to all—that your opinion in a difficult matter is probably the one that is closest to the heart of things.

And unfortunately, you don't usually have enough insight into your own problems. You know the heart of the problem, but you have trouble with the practical details.

You also have difficulty because of your passion for experiencing life's problems firsthand. You don't like advice, you want to find out for yourself. But it doesn't matter because you usuallly repeat the same mistakes over and over anyway.

The chief way to avoid these problems is to keep in contact with the deeper feelings and perceptions you have such ready access to. That is probably why the most successful 7's tend to be sailors, writers and performers. Nature, or expressing your understanding of the world, gives you stability and strength.

8. This is the number of worldly power. Business, especially involving great struggle, even sacrifice, to get to the top is very common. Banking and all kinds of investment are advisable.

You must avoid taking too overbearing an attitude to those around you, however. You must also avoid impatience, both with yourself and with others.

9. This is the number of Mars, the planet of war. Power—sometimes grumpy, frequently destructive—is always your first impulse. Fortunately, you also have the ability to rise above the shortsighted and self-defeating use of power to attain and enjoy much more. For this is also the number of the ideal, of rising from the ashes of failure.

If you listen to your ideals and wake up to your better

self, you attain the very thing you want. It is not unusual for numbers of great power to have some difficulty in finding their better selves. There is so much pressure from within, it is usually easier to get by on power alone rather than on harnessing it for what it was meant for.

You are an odd mixture of generosity and gruffness, tending to be very helpful but having few friends. For the same reason, 9's have fine ideals and plenty of energy but haven't learned the restraint that draws people to them. Fortunately, 9's are very resourceful and usually get it right in the end, when many others have given up.

10. People born on the tenth of the month are similar to 1's. You are just naturally confident in yourself and your point of view. The major difference is that you are more interested in worldly success. Not so much being alone at the top of the heap as simply wielding power is what you find absorbs your interest. There are likely to be many ups and downs.

11. This is a number of tremendous higher vibrations. People born on this date are very high-strung with great swings of mood due to the tremendous forces within. You have the ability to see more than all others. Your best course is always to follow your own intuition, and train yourself to hear it and react to it as if it were law, because for you it is indeed the only law. Learning to understand yourself and your tremendous ideals is the only road to peace and success and what you will call satisfaction. It all comes down to this—nothing else is as important to you as what you decide is important to you.

Others will probably not understand, for you are far ahead of them or above them. This is no more likely to deter you from your course than anything else is, for you are very determined, but there is no reason for you to let it bother you either.

12. Similar to 3's, you people born on the twelfth are rather hard-nosed scrappy types who don't mind a few hard knocks for a little fun or to get things done. You don't even seem to mind a little injury. It's all part of the

game. So you keep plugging away when a lot of others would be home nursing their wounds.

Fresh air and competition suit you well and it is an excellent idea to develop your strength and skills so as to make full use of your rugged potential. To you a little sacrifice goes with the territory.

13. If there is one thing this number is not, it is unlucky. This is probably the luckiest number of the month! People born on this day have a natural talent for success. You just know how to make it all come together for you. Even in the hard times, you get ahead somehow, you get something useful out of it. One reason is your ability to be likable in the exercise of power, and your ability to be powerful in the exercise of your likability.

It all goes together in an easy almost muddling or casual-seeming mastery of organization, of people, of things, of details, whatever. A really fine number.

14. Business deals, money, discussions are the stuff of life to you. You are quick, even tricky, but you also really like the interaction and the challenge of a well-turned deal. You also have a tendency to take risks, to gamble, to make too many deals with too many people. And they are usually the ones who cause the problem. You depend too much on other people coming through or not taking risks themselves. What it really comes down to is this. Your judgment is good but other people don't have such good judgment and will probably make mistakes you wouldn't that will land on your head. But you are resourceful and can work your way out of difficulty usually. Being more careful will probably go a long way for you.

15. This is a powerful number, in some ways similar to 14, but less interested in business and money, more interested in influencing other people. There is considerable magnetism. People seem to recognize your presence, and in case there is any doubt, you can usually convince them very quickly that you are not run-of-the-mill.

You would do very well to concentrate on helping

others, keeping the highest ideals, for that is the way to attain happiness for you. Otherwise, you will find that your great abilities will leave you increasingly disillusioned. You must find tasks worthy of your power. This will make it grow and make you feel as if you have caught life's groove.

16. This is one of the most unusual combinations in the month. People born this day experience two extremes through their life with almost no middle ground. On one hand, you are full of the very feeling of life, the joy of being alive, the energy and fire of it all. You are brave and can even be fierce. On the other hand, you are accident-prone in the extreme and your plans usually come to nothing. These problems are frequently a direct result of your attitude. You just don't plan your moves very carefully, and even when you do plan them and work carefully, you are apt to risk it all on some thoughtless bit of good fun that gets you injured just before the big game.

Unfortunately, this devil-may-care attitude wears you down over the years till you come to expect failure. It might even make you gun-shy.

It isn't impossible to overcome this, just unlikely, because you probably won't want to. But if you do, it's very simple. Enjoy yourself, of course. Just don't waste it on the little stuff, and make sure it's after the game. It's also good to stand up for yourself. Just make sure that there is more in it for you than antagonizing your boss.

17. This is a noble number of peace and strength and good judgment. People born on this date leave a legacy behind, and they have usually earned it. You have a warm, powerful feeling of life, which you communicate to others instantly. You are not always understood on the high plain you wish, but you don't let that stop you from getting things done anyway. That is why you can build so much for the future. Sooner or later, others too will recognize the quality of your work. You are usually not terribly concerned with whether they do or not, im-

mersed as you are in your own fine convictions. A wonderful birthday.

18. People born on the eighteenth usually have a tough road ahead, but fortunately they are extremely determined. In fact, you 18's are usually incapable of giving up. You probably aren't even sure how you would go about giving up even if you decided to. You are similar to people born on the ninth in many ways. The difference is that your ideals are more about large community or national endeavors and your warring nature tends to turn inward. So you have a much larger leap to make from your lower self to your higher self than 9's do. There just isn't enough practice in ordinary life for such large-scale projects as you have a taste for, in order to work your way up to the best expression of your energies. And since so much of your destructive side turned on yourself, you tend to keep away from the community projects and large-scale cooperation that would help you develop.

Your best course is to put aside your personal feelings and work diligently at various community projects until you develop that knack for wielding generosity on the large scale. Without that influence, you will never be happy.

19. This is a number of success, pure and simple. People born on this date usually don't have very many problems. In fact, the problems you see are usually rather simple, and they usually involve questions of how to succeed. Your only negative trait is your tendency to be rather inconsiderate. You don't think enough perhaps about making friends, particularly with strangers. But you will succeed. You are hardworking and get right to the point. And you even have a good time at it.

20. This is the most delightful combination of happiness and sureness of one's self and future. You probably aren't real concerned with things like financial success and getting ahead, but you don't need to be. Quite obviously to you, the best things in life are free. And the next best things probably don't cost too much either. So

you aren't as likely as some to amass power and riches. But you won't tear yourself to pieces, either. In fact, you'll probably have a real good time whatever you do, or don't do. And that's why you feel pretty confident. Besides, your health is likely to be pretty good, too.

21. This number is in many ways the opposite of the previous one. You must fight for what you will get, and you will probably fight for a long time, confronting what will seem like almost insurmountable obstacles, but you will conquer all of them. And you will attain to the greatest heights. You will be rich, famous and honored. If at that point you can relax and take it all in, you will be a happy person indeed.

22. This is the most powerful of all numbers. There are some born on this date whose abilities are almost limitless. They will easily be able to do almost anything they wish, and they will probably set their goals at a level others wouldn't even consider, and then they will reach them. Probably you are not quite that extraordinary, but even if you are an average person born on this date you have abilities far beyond most people.

The drawback to all this power, however, is that it feels like nervous energy and it is very hard to understand it, get a handle on it, tame it and control it. For much of your life you will find yourself swinging between extremes of mood that you, let alone others, can't comprehend. It is extremely important to discipline yourself —always strive for moderation and evenness in your behavior and your habits. This way you will find your tremendous power much easier to control.

It is also good to direct yourself to helping others in the largest possible ways. Humanitarians are frequently 22's who have found that their power was a buried sense of idealism that was so strong it only needed to be recognized to lead its owner to the greatest heights. It is extremely important to avoid the trap of sheer domination that attracts you at an undeveloped stage.

In many ways, this number is like 11, but that number

134

is much more visionary, more concerned with ideas. A 22 looks more to vast projects of a more practical nature. Whatever your future holds, you will find it within you, for you are always your own best judge.

23. This is a good number for speaking, communicating difficult ideas easily. What many would find hard to understand, you people not only can understand but can state in the most direct language. You do tend to get a bit carried away, however. You love to hear yourself talk. And you probably talk loud and forcefully enough for everyone to hear, whether they want to or not.

It is a very good talent, however, for you can always make your way, even when you are not really qualified or ready. You just seem to know what you are talking about. And soon enough, you learn anyway, for you can understand almost anything you set your mind to. You are also good at doing things, learning how things work and using this knowledge instantly. No matter what else happens you can bounce back with abilities like these.

24. This is another number of strength and magnetism. The quiet attraction of an inner warmth coupled with an easygoing strength brings people to you as naturally as breathing. They sense your tolerant attitude and understand at a glance that you aren't a pushover either. You exude trust and loyalty and you expect it in others. Your one real weakness is your very strength. You love peace and devotion and will work hard for it, but you sometimes forget that you can't stake everything on these ideals. When others insist on breaking the harmony, particularly at home, you must be more independent.

Apart from that, you are hardworking and reliable and no dummy, either. You rise quite naturally in business and make few enemies along the way. And you make many friends and admirers.

25. This is the number of wisdom gained through life's experience. People born on this date have a wonderful appreciation of the beauty of life. And you have an open

unselfish attitude about it that leaves a mark on all who come to know you. You are not always appreciated while you are around, but after you leave your impression is indelible. Unfortunately, you wear your heart on your sleeve, and few are willing to be as considerate of you as you are of even the tiniest leaf.

You are also frequently quite deep in your thoughts about life and its mysteries. And again, others, who are almost inevitably more shallow and less caring, will tend to hurt you. This isn't because anybody really wants to hurt you, but because compared to you they are rather thoughtless. But, of course, you understand that.

However, you do learn much from life. It could be said that you are the only ones who truly live all of life, for you learn from the actual living of it, rather than thinking about it. You are that much in touch with this world.

With your experience, your judgment grows, and frequently your fortune, though as often as not your idea of good fortune is simply to be at peace with yourself and the world. And despite what others might say to that, if you do feel that deeply, then you are certainly in harmony with your purpose in life.

26. This is an interesting combination of a great sense of organization and strong tendencies away from it. You have excellent business abilities. You understand and like investment, finances, the long-term building and nurturing on sound footing that makes investment grow. And yet you have trouble finishing anything you start. You have an impulse to get up and walk away from whatever you've begun. You feel restless, antsy. But part of your mind is always fixed on the long term. It's the short term you have trouble with.

And though you like to invest for the future and are unusually capable in planning for the future, appreciating the requirements and necessary pathways, you also spend much of your time brooding about the past. You have trouble getting your mind on the present. And that's where the problem is. You look to past and future, but the here and now makes you want to get up and leave.

You treat your children the same way, planning their futures (you are much too dictatorial by the way) and understanding how much of your own past is reflected in them, and therefore understanding much about them that most parents would miss. But you aren't always in touch with what they want now.

This tendency to split your attention can get strong enough to make you seem unlucky, though you aren't really. It is more an underlying fatalism that you find so attractive that makes it hard for you to take charge of the here and now. Constant practice in ignoring the past and concentrating particularly on the present, finishing everything you can, with the steadiest possible work, will build a tremendous foundation for the future, and one day give you the very past you can most enjoy looking back on.

27. This is another number of power, like 9, but it tends to be less personal. You probably have a real taste for large-scale wielding of power. You want authority, you want to lead, to be looked up to by many people, and you'll work hard to get there.

Up close you may not be the warmest, but you are so little concerned with individual relationships that it doesn't get in the way much. You tend to see life as if you were a picture on a poster advertising your next concert. And the rest of us will probably all stand in line to go.

28. People born on this date are great starters. You have a wonderful view of life. You sense the richness and crispness of things so much you can almost taste the world. You are also likely to be quite smart. The only problem is getting things to work out in the long run the way you would like. You see such a fine view of things at the outset, that it's hard for the end result to match your expectations.

There is also a tendency to rely too much on your brilliant initiative and not prepare adequately. Method, hard work, planning will not detract from you, and you must not feel that your brilliant beginning sense puts you above such considerations. You can attain most anything you want if you do not give up on your good spirits.

29. This is a birthday of contradictions. You have tremendous power. You can rise to the heights of almost anything you undertake, and will probably do so quickly and relatively easily. But your extra energies create a constant pressure you find hard to deal with. Whereas most of the powerful numbers find it difficult to get enough control over their powers to reach their potential, you tend to do it the other way around. Your difficulty is after the success, or apart from it.

You are probably very difficult to live with, though extremely dependent on close personal support. Your nervous energies send you to extremes of mood that embarrass you, confuse you and exhaust you. And you live in a constant tension, trying to keep yourself in balance.

Your tendency to concentrate your attention and energies is the source of both your success and difficulties. You must strive to broaden your interests, and in particular you must try to find more outlets for your nervous energy. Working always to stabilize and soothe your home life is a necessity if you hope to retain your equilibrium.

You may also have discovered your potential for humanitarianism. Helping others is on one hand easy for you, but it is, strangely, a rather stabilizing influence. This is probably because it serves as an outlet for your abilities and also as a boost to your ego, which is itself always tottering between arrogance and insecurity.

30. You have a wonderful versatility, though you probably excel in something artistic. You are sociable, argumentative and generally in good spirits. You have a wonderful imagination but you have a tendency to rely too much on your mental abilities and your stubbornness. There isn't really anything you can't do, but you

don't always get around to doing much of anything sometimes.

Your excellent energies and adaptability are really where the problem starts. You're just too content with your abilities, knowing you will succeed, and therefore not needing to prove it. If you can get yourself focused on doing one thing and trying to succeed in the world, you will probably have a wonderful time.

Your best abilities are generally on the mental plane. Your mind is clear and strong. Artistic endeavors are particularly well suited to you, for you are probably also quite dextrous, though you are not likely to enjoy work that does not require some mental agility.

31. People born on the thirty-first are a blend of the practical and the sensitive. You are very hardworking, in fact you enjoy hard work more than almost anyone. But you have an extreme sensitivity to people, making you one of the most understanding, loyal and long-lasting friends imaginable.

As could be expected of someone who takes so readily to endurance in both work and friendship, you are extraordinarily stubborn. You hold to a position you believe in—be it work, friendship or anything else—and you simply don't quit. You see it through.

Unfortunately, this combination revolves around a very personal idealism that keeps you with few close friends, good friend though you are. You don't move easily in light relationships, and few others are willing to be loyal enough to meet your high standards. Consequently you are probably often lonely. On the other hand, the friendships you do enjoy are much stronger than most other people's.

You tend to worry too much about both food and the future. If you were to lighten up a bit and just work and enjoy for today, you would find that tomorrows tend to come a bit more nicely than you had feared. Don't worry about tomorrow. Work on today. And then, do the same tomorrow.

Now that you know something about the personalities of each birthday, you may have noticed certain similarities throughout the month. There are certain characteristics, themes that keep repeating themselves in varied forms. The reason for that is that there are only nine numbers! And I will show you how to get your number by a simple method called Fadic addition. This is the number you must think of yourself as, in addition to the birth number. Together, they are your lucky numbers, and the numbers you should figure with more than any others. In addition to that, you can take your entire birthday —month, date and year—to get all your lucky numbers. Here's how it's done.

Let's say you were born on the seventeenth. You take the 17 and add the 1 and the 7 together. That's 8.

$$1 + 7 = 8$$

Or suppose you were born on the 24th. Add the 2 and the 4 together.

$$2 + 4 = 6$$

If you were born on the 28th, there's two steps. Add 2 and 8 together.

$$2 + 8 = 10$$

Then add the 1 and the 0 of that 10 together.

$$1 + 0 = 1$$

And that's all there is to it. Add the two numbers together till you get one number. Of course, if you start with one number (if you were born on the third, say) you just leave it at that.

For quick reference, here's a chart.

1	1, 10, 19, 28
2	2, 11, 20, 29
3	3, 12, 21, 30
4	4, 13, 22, 31

```
5   5, 14, 23
6   6, 15, 24
7   7, 16, 25
8   8, 17, 26
9   9, 18, 27
```

So if you were born on the 23rd, you can see that your main lucky numbers are 5 and 23. These are your numbers to think of yourself as, to bet on, to use for choosing a day to plan important meetings on—whatever you can use a lucky number for. Remember, it's always the single digit number, the one on the left-hand column, that is your most important. Unless you were born on the 11th or the 22nd, then your actual birthday number is the most important. And in fact, for people born on the 11th, 22 is also a lucky number; and for people born on the 22nd, 11 is a lucky number.

One of the things you will find useful to you is to compare your birthday with the other birthdays on your line. You will learn more about yourself by reading about them too, since there is a relation between all 5 people, say, or between all 9 people, and so on.

Now, if you want to get all your lucky numbers, you must take your entire birth date. For instance, 10 February 1964.

February is the second month, so we get 10, 2, 1964.

Since 2 is already a single digit, we leave that alone. The 10th day we know from our chart, or from our own addition, is a 1. And 1964 we add radically, just like the birthday—$1 + 9 + 6 + 4 = 20$. And we reduce the 20 to a single digit the same way—$2 + 0 = 2$.

The 10th day is a 1, the 2nd month is a 2, and 1964 is another 2.

The lucky numbers for someone born on this date are 1,2,2.

And don't forget the actual birthday—10.

So the full range of numbers is 1,2,2,10. And the most important of these is the 1 because that is the reduced number for the birth date, which we found in the left-hand column of the chart.

There's one more number you can get, and that is very important also. It is the life path number. You get that by adding your month, birthday, and year all together. So for the above date, 10, 2, 1964, we add them all together and get a 5. That number is the life path number. It is to be read and used like the main lucky number derived from your birthday.

So let's put this all together. If you were born on 16 December 1955, you would know that your main number would come from your birthday. Since that's a 16, we know your main number is 7. You would read about the 16 to learn about yourself, and also read about the other numbers on the same line in the chart (7, 16, 25) to learn a little more. But your everyday lucky number is a 7.

To learn your full range of lucky numbers, we would take the entire birth date—16, 12, 1955. Those numbers, as they are, are useful and can be used whenever you need a long number. Additional numbers can be derived simply by starting the series over: 16, 12, 1955, 16, 12, etc. So if you wanted a twelve digit number, 161219551612 would be excellent.

If, however, you want to find your best numbers in combinations of two or three numbers, you must reduce each of the parts of your birth date by Fadic addition. So you would take 16, 12, 1955; then:

$$16 = 1+6 = 7$$
$$12 = 1+2 = 3$$
$$1955 = 1+9+5+5 = 20 = 2$$

So 732 is your luckiest three digit combination.

And the life path number can be used in the same manner as the everyday lucky number derived from your birthday. To get that, keep adding the numbers Fadically till you get down to a single digit number. In this case, we were at 732. Add them together, we get 12; add the 1 and the 2 of 12 and we get 3. So for someone born on 12 December 1955, the life path number is 3. This number will tell you much about yourself and should be read in conjunction with the birthday reading to determine your total character. Sometimes it can be more important a guide to your personality than the birthday. You shouldn't have any trouble seeing which is the more important of the two and which plays the lesser role. Whichever one is the stronger, use that as your chief number. Think of it as you. Bet on it. Plan on it.

If, however, you find an 11 or 22 in your chart, do not reduce that to a single digit, for those are master numbers and must be used as is. They are extremely powerful. The 22 wields the greatest power of all the numbers, and the 11 is a law unto itself. So if your life path number is either of those, it will surely be more important than your birthday. And if your birthday is either of them, it will surely be the most powerful influence. If you manage to have them on your birthday and your life path too, you already know what extraordinary abilities (and tensions) are yours.

To give you a few examples. Obviously, if you were born on the 11th or the 22nd, you have a master number birthday and should not reduce the 11 to a 2 nor the 22 to a 4. It may be helpful to read the other numbers on the same line in the chart anyway, though with master numbers, there's really no predicting what they'll be like.

If you were born on 10 February 1963, your life path number will add up to 22. $1+0+2+1+9+6+3=22$.

If, however, your birthday adds up to 31, or 13, or 40, than you are a 4.

If your life path number adds up to 20—say, 3 December 1913—your life path is a 2. But if it adds up to 29, 38, 47, etc., or, of course, to an 11, then you are an 11.

These numbers can play a big part in your life. They

143

can be used to learn more about yourself and the people you know. You can even have an idea of what strangers will be like. If you can find out the birth date of a prospective employer, for instance, you'll have some idea of what he will consider important in people he hires.

And, of course, it can be very useful to know which numbers—whether they be days, addresses, bets or lotteries—are the luckiest for you.

In any case, use your numbers as if they were a part of you: think of them, identify with them, make them your own.